Stereotypes of Muslim Women in the United States

Stereotypes of Muslim Women in the United States

Media Primes and Consequences

Alexis Tan
Anastasia Vishnevskaya

LEXINGTON BOOKS
Lanham • Boulder • New York • London

Published by Lexington Books
An imprint of The Rowman & Littlefield Publishing Group, Inc.
4501 Forbes Boulevard, Suite 200, Lanham, Maryland 20706
www.rowman.com

86-90 Paul Street, London EC2A 4NE, United Kingdom

British Library Cataloguing in Publication Information Available

Library of Congress Cataloging-in-Publication Data
Names: Tan, Alexis S., author. I Vishnevskaya, Anastasia, author.
Title: Stereotypes of Muslim women in the United States : media primes and
   consequences / Alexis Tan and Anastasia Vishnevskaya.
Description: Lanham, Maryland : Lexington Books, [2022] I Includes bibliographical
   references and index. I Summary: "This book presents evidence that verbal and visual
   symbols in the media can activate implicit prejudices towards Muslim women in the
   United State and that social liberals, not social conservatives, can control activation.
   Authors suggest media and intrapersonal interventions to mitigate the harmful
   consequences of gendered Islamophobia"—Provided by publisher.
Identifiers: LCCN 2022014220 (print) I LCCN 2022014221 (ebook) I ISBN
   9781793628350 (cloth) I ISBN 9781793628367 (epub)
Subjects: LCSH: Muslim women—United States—Public opinion. I Islamophobia—
   United States. I Stereotypes (Social psychology)—United States.
Classification: LCC HQ1170 .T37 2022 (print) I LCC HQ1170 (ebook) I DDC
   305.48/6970973—dc23/eng/20220329
LC record available at https://lccn.loc.gov/2022014220
LC ebook record available at https://lccn.loc.gov/2022014221

♾™ The paper used in this publication meets the minimum requirements of American
National Standard for Information Sciences—Permanence of Paper for Printed Library
Materials, ANSI/NISO Z39.48-1992.

Anastasia:
To Natali, Andrey, Vasiliy, and Simon
Alex:
To Gerdean, Riz, Marco, and Deb

Contents

Acknowledgments

We thank Jessie Tepper and her colleagues at Lexington Books for making this book possible, Heena Khan for her collaboration on two studies, Di Mu for helping with the figures, and Saba Siddique for the photographs we used in the third study.

ANASTASIA

I am very grateful to Alex Tan for the opportunity to work on this project and for being such a supportive mentor and advisor whose help and encouragement made it possible to complete this book.

A very special thanks to my parents and my brother for their love and support and to Misty and Robert Springer and the rest of their family for always being there for me.

Last but not least, thank-you to Christy Curtis, Jason McConnell, Joseph Navelski, Jerry Stott, and Rachel Wong for keeping me going. This book is very much their accomplishment as well as ours.

ALEX

My appreciation to Anastasia Vishnevskaya, equal coauthor, whose knowledge of online experimental designs was invaluable and whose competent work and persistence kept us going. Also, thank you to the scholars we cite and Muslim women everywhere. And not to be forgotten, thanks to my family for their support and encouragement.

Chapter 1

Introduction

This book fills a gap in the research literature about stereotypes of Muslim women in the United States. We discuss these stereotypes and how they are activated; present a theoretical model that identifies media primes, antecedents, and consequences of stereotype activation; identify interventions that mitigate the harmful effects of stereotyping Muslim women; and discuss three original studies that test propositions of stereotype activation control. While a large body of research about Muslim women exists in Western Europe, Muslim women have largely been overlooked in the United States. They occupy a unique space in American culture and politics, considering the 9/11 attacks on the United States and increased anti-Muslim rhetoric and the implementation of anti-Muslim policies during the Trump administration (Bridge Initiative, 2017).

Since 9/11 and the escalation of the US war on terror in Afghanistan in 2001, the complex public and media perceptions of Muslim women in the United States have placed Muslim women at the center of political discourse seeking to provide a rationale for rampant Islamophobia. On the one hand, Muslim women, much like their male counterparts, are portrayed by the media and perceived by the public to be cultural threats: their values, way of life, beliefs and religion, perceived support for violence and terrorism counter Western culture and therefore should be prevented from contaminating mainstream cultures in the United States and Western European countries. As a consequence, many of these countries have imposed strict restrictions on immigration and travel from Muslim countries (e.g., Bridge Initiative, 2017; Saleem et al., 2017). The other side of perceptions of Muslim women sees them as oppressed, unwilling victims of misogynistic and patriarchal Islamic cultures who must be liberated from oppressive and barbaric Islamic regimes ruled by men such as the Taliban (Janson, 2011).

This view is often used as a rationale for the war on terror and vigilance against Muslim terrorism (Sides & Gross, 2013).

On the one hand, then, Muslim women are perceived as a cultural threat; on the other, they are allies in the movement toward the liberation of women. Regardless of which perception is held, Muslim women fit into what Edward Said called the tyranny of Orientalism (Said, 1978), forever the mysterious out-group. To rationalize colonization of foreign cultures, Western countries created the myth of the "other"—colonized people, because they were "different," deserved a better life, one that could be offered by the colonizers. In today's context, Muslim women provide a convenient tool for the rationalization of general bias toward Muslims and Islam. They are different, but do not wish to be so. Therefore, they should be liberated. The picture of Muslim women in most Western countries, reinforced by images in the media, as oppressed, passive, and unwilling participants in the Islamization of the world is a major instrument in Western cultivation of Islamophobia, albeit not the only picture. This distorted picture of Islam as presented in Western countries is described by Mahmoud (2002, as cited in Janson, 2011):

> women wearing headscarves (now, *burqas*), the cutting off of hands and heads, and massive crowds praying in unison, the imposition of a normative public morality grounded in a puritanical and legalistic interpretation of religious texts, a rejection and hatred of the West and its globalized culture, the desire to put aside history and return to a pristine past, and the quick recourse to violence against those who are different. (p. 348)

The premise of this book is that the voices of Muslim women in the United States have not been heard often enough in the research literature. How do they perceive themselves, as compared to Western public and media perceptions? What are the effects of public and media perceptions on their daily lives, and on life-changing experiences such as employment and hate crimes? What interventions might mitigate negative effects of these perceptions? Our objective is to provide a voice to Muslim women in the United States by providing some answers based on social science research. Some of this research is in the United States. Most studies are in Western Europe. We discuss results regardless of origin and apply findings to shared and unique experiences.

Much of the research on Muslims has looked at public perceptions connecting terrorism to Islam. Few have distinguished between Muslim men and women. An argument can be made that Muslim men and women experience prejudice and discrimination differently. Therefore, these experiences should be discussed separately. For example, a 2017 Pew Research Center survey in the United States of a random sample of Muslim women showed that significantly more Muslim women than Muslim men said that they had experienced at least one incidence of discrimination in the past year (56% women, 42% men). These incidents included: "people have acted as if they are suspicious of you" (34% W, 29% M); "have been called offensive names" (26% W, 13% M); "have been singled out by airport security" (21% W, 16% M); "have been physically threatened or attacked" (6% W; 6% M). Additionally, Muslim women were more likely than Muslim men to say that "U.S. media coverage of Muslims is unfair" (68% W, 52% M); "there is a lot of discrimination against Muslims in the U.S." (83% W, 68% M); "It has been more difficult to be Muslim in the U.S. in recent years" (57% W; 43% M); "the GOP is unfriendly toward Muslim Americans" (69% W; 49% M); and "Trump is unfriendly toward Muslim Americans" (81% W, 68% M) (Pew Research Center, 2017). These data suggest that American Muslim women perceive their experiences in the US to be significantly more negative than do American Muslim men.

An explanation might be the implicit association of all Muslims (and Islam) with cultural and physical threats to American society (Ciftci, 2012). Women are more easily identified as Muslims when they wear the veil, head covering (hijab) and dress covering the entire body (burqa). Therefore, their identities as Muslim activate negative stereotypes particularly those labeling them as threats to "true Americans." About half of Muslim women in the US say, "something about their appearance identifies them as Muslim" (Pew Research Center, 2017). Muslim women, therefore, deserve special attention in any discussion of prejudice against Muslims. Their experiences are more negative compared to men, and they are more easily associated with Islam by their attire.

A basic theoretical assumption of our book is that most negative biases and prejudices toward Muslim women are held implicitly (unconsciously) by non-Muslims and are activated by primes—symbols in the environment including in traditional and social media. We have structured the book around priming theory as an explanation of how implicit biases and stereotypes are activated to trigger discriminatory evaluations and behaviors. We ask the following questions:

1. What are public stereotypes in the United States about Muslim women? How do these stereotypes relate to stereotypes about Muslims in general? What is the role of media in the formation of stereotypes of Muslim women? *Chapter 2 (Historical and Current Stereotypes of Muslim Women in the United States and the Role of the Media in Their Formation)* addresses these questions, discusses how these stereotypes have evolved since 9/11, and suggests that stereotypes of Muslim women are key components of gendered Islamophobia, fear of Muslim women because of religion and gender.

2. What is public opinion in the United States about Muslim women? What are the consequences of stereotypes of Muslim women on their personal lives? *Chapter 3 (Public Opinion in the United States and the Consequences of Muslim Women Stereotypes)* provides evidence of pre-dominantly negative public opinion and stereotypes of Muslim women in the United States. Drawing from priming theory, chapter 3 explains how negative public stereotypes of Muslim women can negatively impact their personal lives.

3. How does priming theory explain media influence on stereotyping of Muslim women? *Chapter 4 (Priming and Activation Control of Stereotypes)* presents a priming model of the activation and application of implicit stereotypes and applies the model to stereotypes of Muslim women. Because most negative stereotypes of Muslim women are implicit, chapter 4 suggests that priming theory is a more powerful explanation than cognitive models of prejudice. Activation control is a prominent feature of our model. As research on prejudice has recently moved toward explaining bias control, we suggest how bias toward Muslim women can be controlled so that discriminatory responses can be avoided.

4. What are the consequences of primed negative stereotypes of Muslim women? Why are Muslim women easily identifiable primes? Who in a mainstream audience are more likely to be influenced by primes? *Chapter 5 (Priming Negative Stereotypes of Muslim Women: Antecedents and Consequences)* identifies semantic and visual primes in the environment, including religious attire, that activate negative stereotypes of Muslim women. Chapter 5 provides evidence of the negative effects of primed stereotypes such as aggression, hate crimes, and employment discrimination. How do Muslim women respond to acts of hate and aggression? What coping mechanisms do they use? We present a theoretical framework that identifies groups in a mainstream population (e.g., White Americans) who are most likely to apply activated negative stereotypes to aggression, hate crimes, and discriminatory behaviors.

5. What are the conditions when priming and activation control occur? *Chapter 6 (Semantic and Visual Primes of Stereotypes of Muslim Women: Activation and Activation Control)* presents three studies that investigate when and how priming and activation control occur. We study negative stereotypes of Muslim women primed by religious attire and their differential effects on college students, American adults who are not college students, and liberals and conservatives.

6. How can activated negative stereotypes of Muslim women be controlled so that they do not result in hate crimes, aggressions, and discriminatory evaluations and actions? *Chapter 7 (Interventions Applied to Muslim*

Women) presents strategies for controlling harmful effects of activated negative stereotypes. Drawing from research on prejudice interventions, we discuss how proactive interventions initiated by the individual and reactive interventions initiated by the media can prevent harmful behaviors from activated negative stereotypes. Examples are enhancing motivations for activation control, enhancing empathy, priming counter-stereotypes, and balanced narratives.

7. *Chapter 8 (Conclusions and Recommendations)* elaborates on a model of activation control as an intervention. Key elements of this model are individual differences, information processing, and affective and behavioral components of bias. The model suggests that research on activation control and priming should account for these variables. We conclude that Muslim women in the United States, similar to their counterparts in Western Europe, Canada, New Zealand, and Australia, are victims of gendered Islamophobia but their victimization can be countered by activation control of stereotypes and their application.

Chapter 2

Historical and Current Stereotypes of Muslim Women in the United States and the Role of the Media in Their Formation

In this chapter, we discuss the evolving content of public stereotypes on Muslim women, particularly, pre– and post–9/11 stereotypes, and the role of the mass media in their formation. Muslim women stereotypes have been studied extensively in Canada (e.g., Bullock & Jafri, 2002), New Zealand (e.g., Rahman, 2020), and European countries such as France (e.g., Abdeslam, 2020; Hennig, 2021), Germany (e.g., Dioulgkaridou, 2021), Spain (Calvo-Barbero & Carrasco-Campos, 2020), and the Netherlands (e.g., van Es, 2019). Muslim stereotypes and their implications for Muslim women continue to be studied in these countries from a variety of theoretical perspectives (critical and social science) and methodologies (quantitative and qualitative). In this chapter, we will be focusing on historical and current stereotypes of Muslim women in the United States. Muslim women have largely been overlooked by American scholars, who have emphasized other American racial minorities.

CURRENT STEREOTYPES OF MUSLIM WOMEN

Bullock and Jafri (2002; see also Posetti, 2007; Perry, 2014) group the stereotypes of Muslim women into three general categories: a "harem belly-dancer character" or a "sexualized woman of the 'Orient'", an "oppressed Muslim woman," and finally—a "militant Muslim woman" (p. 36). Below, we will discuss each of these three stereotypical groups more in depth.

A Sexualized Woman of the Orient

Muslim women are sexualized to the extent that their value is reduced to their bodies (Perry, 2014). Historically, this has been the case, and it remains true up until today—Muslim women bodies are "silent, inscrutable objects of desire" (Agathangelou & Ling, 2004, p. 528; see also Ling, 1999). Muslim women are depicted as strikingly beautiful and exotic. Such depiction makes their bodies more tempting, but simultaneously exacerbates the difference in beauty standards between Western and Eastern women, and thus further perpetuates the concept of "us" and "them" (Perry, 2014). The presence of veil in Muslim women images goes both ways: it exacerbates the idea of Otherness, and it also serves as both a captivating and frightening element in Muslim women's portrayals (Perry, 2014). The presence of veil perpetuates the allure; it also induces sexualized fantasies about what is hidden behind it (Ibid).

The idea of exoticization of Muslim women bodies is tied to the colonialization of Muslim societies (see Brown, 2006). Bhabha (1994) explains the psychology behind such perception: "[the colonized body] is always simultaneously . . . inscribed in both the economy of pleasure and desire and the economy of discourse, domination and power" (p. 67). The cultural element of Muslim societies—harem—has also contributed to the perpetuation of the image of Muslim women bodies as exotic and alluring (see Macdonald, 2006). The image of Muslim women in harem is associated with sexual fantasy and mystique anticipation, thus increasing the fascination of women's veils. Naficy (2003) asserts that the element of veil helps to sexualize and objectify women bodies, which "turn the objects of the look into eroticized subjects" (p. 141).

However, the nature of harem as an only-women space perpetuates the misperception of Muslim societies as barbaric, where women are intentionally excluded from social interactions, and the image of women as repressed and submissive (Macdonald, 2006).

Oppressed Muslim Women

Milinkovic (2014) explains that Islam is often perceived as a religion where women are oppressed. Muslim women are often described as "passive, submissive, inactive, and highly dependent on others" (Jawad & Benn, 2003, pp. 9–10). This dependency and submissiveness are often attributed to male representatives of the Muslim culture and religion—husbands, brothers, or other family members (Perry, 2014). Such oppression is also portrayed as a cultural norm in Muslim societies (Ibid).

Muslim women stereotypes are closely tied to their attire. The cover—hijab, veil, burqa, or other types of female religious and cultural covers—is an attribute of Islamic religion and culture, but it is also attributed to Muslim women's sociocultural positioning, the lack of their agency and the presence of oppression toward them (e.g., Macdonald, 2006; Abdeslam, 2020).

The scholarship over the past years focuses more and more on the presence of Muslims in Western societies and exploring mainly the issues of facial covers (the veil) and/or securitization in these societies (Moors & Tarlo, 2013). Such dress practices are perceived to be a threat to Western values and draw attention to the need for restrictions on them in the defense of secular society and [Western] women's rights (Moors & Tarlo, 2013).

While Muslim men are associated with war, terror, and fanaticism, Muslim women are found in need of rescue and liberation by the West (Maira, 2011). Especially after 9/11, the long-term stereotypes of Muslim women as oppressed, weak, and helpless creatures who are controlled by their religious beliefs became prominent in Western societies (Eltantawy, 2007). Moreover, the veil remained as a "static colonial image that symbolizes Western superiority over Eastern backwardness" (Razak, 2008, p. 120).

Muslim's women cover symbolizes perceived oppression. However, it simultaneously increases the risk of violence, which is often Islamophobic violence (Kwan, 2008). The veil reinforces the sense of Otherness and further alienates Muslim women from Western women (Eltantawy, 2007).

The weakness of Muslim women and oppression toward them was, however, a portrayal of reality that perpetuated violence against Muslims in general and helped to justify military actions in the Middle East after 9/11 to liberate the Muslim women from their oppressors (e.g., Perry, 2014). Simultaneously, veiled women are not only to be saved and liberated, to be respected, to be educated, but also to be feared because they were often perceived to be willing and unwilling accomplices of "terrorist Muslim men" (Wagner et al., 2012; see also Ahmed, 1992; Dwyer, 1999; Secor, 2002).

Muslim Women as Terrorists

The last most common stereotypical image of Muslim women is a perception of Muslim women as terrorists. This stereotype is tied to the Muslim women's veil and the fact of hidden unknown behind it (see Perry, 2014). However, in this case, the veil is not a symbol of oppression anymore but is rather a symbol of Islamic aggression. Stereotypical portrayal of Muslim women as terrorists, especially if they are covered, implies their representation as "mysterious, dangerous, and threatening" (Perry, 2014, p. 83). This fact is especially interesting and reveals a stereotypical paradox of Muslim women portrayals, which implies that Muslim women wearing a veil can be either exotic and mysterious or they can be mysterious and threatening (Ibid). Nahid Kabir (2004) also shows that veiled Muslim women are often depicted in the media as violent and threatening to public security (see also Issaka, 2021).

Jiwani (2005), analyzing the Canadian *Globe and Mail*'s reports on Middle Eastern military actions after 9/11, revealed the stereotypical coverage of Muslim women as terrorists and warriors, alongside with male Muslim terrorists. In those coverage, Muslim women were described as "mothers of suicide bombers," which emphasizes even more gender differences between Muslim and Western women (Jiwani, 2005, p. 17). While Western women can be "real" mothers, Muslim women are different—they are violent and barbarian (Perry, 2014; also see Jiwani, 2005).

The active recruitment of Muslim women by Islamic terrorist groups, often reported in Western media, solidifies the stereotype of Muslim women as threatening terrorists (Laster & Erez, 2015). Existing gender stereotypes reinforce stereotypes of Muslim women as "Muslim women-terrorists." Muslim women are perceived by the public to be actively used in terrorist roles due to their perceived femininity—weakness and helplessness, submissive and nurturing nature. Given these feminine characteristics, they are unlikely to be perceived as potential terrorists themselves unlike Muslim men (see Organization for Security and Co-operation in Europe [OECD], 2012, p. 3). As a result, women terrorists have an element of unpredictability in their military actions (Cook, 2005), which makes them more threatening for the mainstream society.

All of these three stereotypical groups are based on gendered Islamophobia, which is defined as "the fear, hatred, and/or discrimination against Muslim women based on Orientalist ideology that typifies Muslim women as oppressed, exotic, and dangerous" (as cited in Swisher, 2019; see also Hammer, 2013; Perry, 2014; Zine, 2006). Gendered Islamophobia includes general stereotypes of women, such as, for instance, women are usually less powerful, more economically and socially marginalized in comparison to men (as cited in Essers & Benschop, 2009; Predelli, 2004). However, the key component of gendered Islamophobia that exacerbates gender violence and crime against Muslim women is religion (see Perry, 2014). Muslim women—unlike Western women—more often find themselves under the pressure of rethinking their activities, habits, reconsidering their experiences and place in society not only due to their gender but mainly due to their religion (Perry, 2014, p. 85).

THE EVOLUTION OF STEREOTYPES
ABOUT MUSLIM WOMEN POST-9/11

Prior to the attacks of 9/11, more than 50% of the American respondents who participated in a Roper survey agreed that Islam was "inherently anti-American, anti-Western or supportive of terrorism" even though only 5% of the respondents had any personal interaction with a Muslim individual

(Blank, 1998, p. 22; also see Barkdull et al., 2011). This public opinion toward Muslims was most likely shaped by Western media that for a long time have portrayed Muslims as violent and aggressive terrorists and barbarians (e.g., Alsultany, 2012; Dixon & Williams, 2015; Nacos, Nacos & Torres-Reyna, 2007; Powell, 2011), and it has been established in communication scholarship that media does have an effect on public opinion (e.g., Entman, 1989, 1993).

Ahmed and Matthes (2017) in their recently conducted meta-analysis on *Media representation of Muslims and Islam from 2000 to 2015* argue that after 9/11 the representation of Muslims in the mainstream media remained negative (see also Brown, 2006), but now the media started putting more emphasis on the content of religious extremism (see Kumar, 2010; El-Aswad, 2013). Undoubtedly, media played a significant role in perpetuating such stereotypes, mainly to align those with the geopolitical interests of the Bush administration (e.g., Kellner, 2004; Ahmed & Matthes, 2017). For instance, prominent media sources as the *New York Times* (Mishra, 2007), the *Los Angeles Times* and the *Washington Post* (Trevino et al., 2010), and CNN (Martin & Phelan, 2002) were verbally and visually portraying Muslims as "terrorists," "extremists," "fundamentalists," and "fanatics." Such rhetoric helped the US government to frame and justify the war on terror to its domestic audience (Issaka, 2021).

At the same time, the events of 9/11 also contributed significantly to the public stereotypes of Muslim women, especially the women who wear veils. For instance, Kaya (2007) observed that the visibility of Muslim women due to their veiling increased their vulnerability to physical and verbal forms of violence as veiled women were associated with terrorists and extremists. Covered Muslim women were a visual reminder to the American public that the Islamic culture was present in their society (Badr, 2004).

Many Americans started associating the Muslim women's religious and/ or cultural cover with the image of the enemy (Yazbeck Haddad, 2007), the terrorist groups that have declared war on the United States. As a result, women, due to their visibility (e.g., Issaka, 2021), became an easier target than Muslim men for harassment and violence. The American public would judge Muslim women for their "choices" to be oppressed, whereas common catcalls such as "Death to Muslims," "America is for Americans," and "I hate you," would force Muslim women to stay home to avoid the public defamation (Yazbeck Haddad, 2007, p. 263).

ROLE OF THE MEDIA IN THE FORMATION OF STEREOTYPES TOWARD MUSLIMS

The stereotypes of Muslim women in the United States and other Western countries develop not so much out of personal contact (few Americans have personal contact with Muslim women), but from the biased media coverage.

News media is an essential and powerful tool for distributing information to the target audiences (e.g., Chomsky, 1997; Entman, 1989, 1993). News media also plays a role in shaping public opinion (e.g., Milinkovic, 2014; McCombs & Valenzuela, 2020), public discourse on issues (e.g., Van Dijk, 1995), and contributes to the formation of stereotypes (e.g., Brummett, 2014; Dixon, 2019). Depending on the medium that shares these messages, the effect of such messages varies (e.g., Barker & Galasinski, 2001). For instance, messages shared through TV or print media or radio will all have different effects on their recipients (Milinkovic, 2014, p. 10; see also Barker & Galasinski, 2001, p. 8).

The extent to which media impact the target audience is also determined by the extent to which this audience relies on the media for information. For instance, La Ferle et al. (2005) argue that media-dominated societies, such as the United States, rely a lot on media portrayals of the events that people do not experience themselves. Thus, the American audience's perceptions of the real world will be determined by the messages and images shared by the media (e.g., Fleras & Kunz, 2001; Henry & Tator, 2002; see also Hirji, 2011).

Public perceptions about Muslims in the United States are derived from media portrayals (Watt, 2012). However, these portrayals are not necessarily accurate and are often biased with political implications (e.g., Amz, 2014). Studies show that media depict minority groups, including Muslims, as a threat and a burden to their host societies (e.g., Abrajano & Singh, 2009; Baum, 2003; Branton & Dunaway, 2008; Entman, 1990; Gilliam & Iyengar, 2000; Gilliam et al., 1996; Iyengar, Peters, & Kinder, 1982; Kellstedt, 2005; Prior, 2005; Wortley, Hagan, & Macmillan, 1997). Media also perpetuates the creation of the idea of Otherness and exclusion of these minority groups from their host societies (e.g., Gilliam & Iyengar, 2000; Kellstedt, 2003, 2005; van Dijk, 1995). Finally, mass media play a role in communicating dominant social values, ideologies, and developments (Ahmed & Matthes, 2017) and thus often contribute to stereotypical portrayals of minorities (Hall, 1990, 1992; Saha, 2012; Van Dijk, 1991).

Lajevardi (2021) argues that stereotypical portrayals of Muslims as threatening and violent are not new and existed prior to the events of 9/11 (e.g., Behm-Morawitz & Ortiz, 2013; Esposito, 1999; GhaneaBassiri, 2013; Said, 1979; Selod, 2015; Shaheen, 2003; Steet, 2000; Wilkins, 1995). However, emphasis of these stereotypes increased significantly in news and entertainment after the terrorist attacks of 9/11 (Bleich & van der Veen, 2020; Nacos & Torres-Reyna, 2002, 2007) with increased portrayals of Muslims as terrorists. The media have turned into tools for demonization of Muslims to help the American government justify the war on terror for the American public (Gadarian, 2010, p. 469; see also Behm-Morawitz & Ortiz, 2013; Merolla & Zechmeister, 2009). As a result, US media deliberately and unintentionally helped to create the discourse of the "global terrorism" and promote this agenda to the rest of the world (Amz, 2014).

After the events of September 11, 2001, Western media created negative images of Muslims worldwide including in the United States. For instance, some media sources used caricatures of Arabs and Muslims portraying them as mad religious figures or depicting them in cartoons with bombs in their turbans (Bowman, 2006). With increased frequency, media depicted airplane hijackings, skyscraper terrorism, and suicide bombers. Overall, these negative images of Islam in the Western media collectively presented Islam and all Muslims as threats to Western societies (Varisco, 2005; Richardson, 2004; see also El-Aswad, 2013).

MEDIA STEREOTYPES OF MUSLIM WOMEN

The terrorist attacks of 9/11 drew increased media attention to the Middle East. For instance, the US media started to extensively cover Muslim societies and Arab and Muslim women. The coverage of Muslim women in their societies was generally one-sided, as, for example, violence of the Taliban regime toward their women (see Yazbeck Haddad, 2007).

The overall stereotypical representation of Muslim women in the Western media has not changed much after the events of 9/11. US media continued to maintain the stereotypes of oppression and threat (e.g., Zahedi, 2011). These stereotypes are exacerbated by the increased visibility of Muslims in American society. Some Muslim women, for example, wear the veil, a religious and/or cultural cover making the identities of Muslim women easily noticeable (Selod & Embrick, 2013). The visibility of the veil perpetuated further stereotyping of Muslim women in the media; hijab or the veil facilitated media portrayals of Muslim women as either extremists and terrorists or as oppressed creatures that need to be saved, reinforcing stereotypes discussed earlier in this chapter.

US news coverage of Muslim women is often driven by "confirmation bias" (e.g., Terman, 2017). American journalists, in news stories in the *New York Times* and *Washington Post*, are more likely to report on women living in fundamentalist Muslim countries, focusing on the "Muslim women oppressed" theme, the violation of women rights, and gender inequalities, thus further reinforcing popular public stereotypes about these women (Ibid). Abdeslam (2020) also notes that news stories often reinforce portrayals of Muslim women as helpless victims of honor-based violence.

The portrayals of Muslim women in American news are similar to such portrayals in the US entertainment media. For instance, Steinberg (2002) emphasizes that the Hollywood portrays "Arabs and Middle Easterners in exotic ethnic terms" (p. 206) (as cited in Arti, 2007). Hirji (2011) also argues that since 9/11 the portrayals of Muslim women did not evolve. On the contrary, such shows as for instance *Little Mosque on the Prairie* further perpetuated images of Muslim women as exotic and sexualized objects and oppressed victims. Reporter Carol Memmott (2004) also wrote about the plight of Muslim women "who live under the restrictions of Islam" (p. 4D) (as cited in Eltantawy, 2007).

Islam in general is presented in most American media as a threatening culture and religion. Such generalizations further perpetuate portrayals of covered Muslim women in need of liberation (see Rahmath, Chambers & Wakewich, 2016). Eventually, these portrayals of Muslim women as victims of their own religion and culture and as being "oppressed," contributes to the Western public perception that Islam is a threatening religion and culture, as presented by the dominant media stereotypes (see García et al., 2011; also Calvo-Barbero & Carrasco-Compos, 2020).

Women as Oppressed

Barkdull et al. (2011) emphasize that Muslim women are often stereotyped in US media as "veiled, submissive, and oppressed" (p. 140). Such stereotypical portrayals omit the understanding of "the intricate role of state institutions and historical, social, political, and regional factors" in societies where Muslim women live (Critelli, 2010, p. 236). The media also presents Muslim women as sexually objectified and oppressed by authoritarian Muslim men. Women are portrayed as passive, with no agency in determining their own life. They are often portrayed as suffering from honor-based violence (see Abdeslam, 2020). These portrayals reinforce "the classic narrative of helpless Muslim women destined to suffer at the hands of misogynist Muslim men until rescued by enlightened, compassionate Westerners" (Green, 2015, p. 242).

Popular media outlets portray Muslim societies as sexist and lacking gender equality norms. Such portrayals affect the perception of Islamic culture overall, representing it as biased and discriminatory against women (see Ahmad, 2009; Bahramitash, 2005; Mahmood, 2009). Such representation is inaccurate and incomplete and does not explain the totality of women's experiences in Muslim cultures (Abu-Lughod, 2013). Instead, these stereotypical portrayals continue further demonizing Muslim societies (Bhattacharyya, 2008; Puar, 2007), their patriarchal structures, and the lack of Muslim women's agency (Mahmood, 2011; Terman, 2017).

The reinforcement of Muslim women images as oppressed and submissive in the US media also serves as a justification for US political actions toward Muslims (e.g., Mahmood, 2009; Maira, 2009; Razack, 2008; Terman, 2017). Media portrayals of Muslim women identities after 9/11 are found within the frames of both racial and gender politics. As a result, media discourse of liberation of Muslim women focuses on the liberation of these women from either ideological extremism or from racism and Islamophobia (see Zine, 2006; Calvo-Barbero & Carrasco-Compos, 2020).

Media stereotypes of Muslims as a cultural threat are reinforced by US media and tie the discourses of Muslim women and gender inequality (see Terman, 2017). For instance, after 9/11, American media has heavily increased the coverage of Muslim women in Afghanistan (e.g., Cloud, 2004; Fowler, 2013; Hirschkind & Mahmood, 2002; Klaus & Kassel, 2005; Shepherd, 2006). Such coverage emphasized atrocities that Muslim women faced from men. The extensive emphasis on Taliban women's sufferings justified to the American audience the necessity of the US presence in the Middle East—to "save" these Muslim women and to bring Western societal norms and values to their culture. Among such norms and values were gender equality and respect for women (Milinkovic, 2014). Even American and British political leaders' wives—Laura Bush and Cherie Blair, respectively—joined the discourse, referring to Afghan women as deprived of human rights under the Taliban regime, needing freedom from their male counterparts and education (Barker & Galasinski, 2001, p. 6; Ward, 2001).

Veil as a Symbol of Oppression

Media representations are central to creating common-sense understandings of a wide range of social events and issues (Altheide, 2000; Gamson et al., 1992). Veiling by Muslim women in Western nations is a common representation of Muslim women (see Byng, 2010).

The oppressed image of Muslim women is reinforced in Western societies by images in the media of women wearing head scarves (hijabs) and clothing covering the whole body (burqas). These images reinforce stereotypes of Muslim women as out-groups, fundamentalists, and threats to Western culture, reinforcing perceptions that they are "different" and "don't fit in" (e.g., Janson, 2011.) These generalized perceptions have led to public policies in some Western countries regulating the wearing of hijabs and burqas. For example, Belgium banned wearing hijabs and veils in public in 2010; France in 2014 banned wearing visible "religious symbols" including hijabs in state schools (Janson, 2011).

While there are numerous reasons for Muslim women to wear the veil, the representation made by the Western media remains unchanged over time (see Perry, 2014). Many Western countries consider veils, hijabs, and burqas as "different" and as a threat to their native cultures, symbols of Islam and ideologies that support terrorism. Because of these associations, Muslim women are often the targets of verbal and physical hate crimes rooted in

Islamophobia (e.g., Soltani, 2016). Pintak, Bowe and Albright (2019), for example, report threatening threats in social media to Deeda Abboud, a candidate for the Democratic nomination for Senate in Arizona in the 2018 primaries: "Wrap that towel around your neck." "Time for target practice."

It is also important to note that the veil has become "[a] standard symbol for the oppression of women in the Western media" (Green, 2015, p. 242). It is also presented by the Western media as a symbol of backwardness and the uncivilized nature of Islam (Abdeslam, 2020). While some scholars describe veil as an alluring object with no specific identifier of cultural ties (e.g., El Guindi, 1999, p. 10), to a larger extent the veil is a symbolic representation of oppression and is strongly perceived as visualization of Islam (see Macdonald, 2006).

As it has been noted before, the stereotypes of Muslim women wearing the veil existed prior to the 9/11. The events of 9/11 did not create new stereotypes, but rather strengthened already existing ones. For instance, Watson (1994) asserted that "the image of a veiled Muslim woman seems to be one of the most popular Western ways of representing the 'problems of Islam'" (p. 153). However, while the ability of the Muslim women's veil to trigger hostile emotions and perpetuate further discussion about Muslim women's place in Islamic culture (see Macdonald, 2006), the extensive focus on Muslim women veiling/unveiling is also argued to be destructing for the understanding of the true underlying political and economic reasons of Muslim women's repression (e.g., El Saadawi, 1980).

Women as a Threat

Women that wear any sort of religious or cultural facial cover, such as veil, burqa, or hijab, are simultaneously perceived as oppressed, exotic, and threatening. Such perceptions are common in Western societies and are reinforced heavily by media sources. Media coverage often contains stories about war and terror and atrocities toward women in Muslim societies. A number of studies explored media portrayals and perception of hijab usage by Muslim women (e.g., Fahmy, 2004). While veil can often be seen as an object of exoticism (e.g., Donnell, 2003), the events of 9/11 shifted the perception of veil mainly in one direction. Veil became a "xenophobic, more specifically Islamophobic lens through which the veil, or headscarf, is seen as a highly visible sign of a despised difference" (Donnell, 2003, p. 123).

These media stories also often contain photos of veiled women, which are not necessarily visualizing the content of the story itself (Jiwani, 2005; Falah, 2005; Kassam, 2008; MacDonald, 2006). However, the context behind the photos is rarely provided. Thus, the interpretation of the meaning of veiled women on the images that usually accompany articles on war, terror, and atrocities, is often left for the target audience (see in Watt, 2012).

The image of veiled Muslim women also perpetuates the concept of Otherness, making Muslim and Arab women visually more distinct from Western women, thus solidifying the stereotype of "the other woman" (SibAi, 2014). Al-Saji (2010) argues that the stereotypical portrayals of Muslim veiled women through the lens of Western media does not truly reflect Muslim women but rather creates an image that allows the Western construction of gender identity to look comparatively better. Thus, often covered Muslim woman are portrayed as victims but also as a manifestation of outdated and extremist cultural traditions (Lamrabet, 2014; Valdés-Peña, 2013). This perspective makes the veil a symbol of Islam and projects the impact of Islamic culture on Muslim and Western societies (see Calvo-Barbero & Carrasco-Compos, 2020).

Chapter 3

Public Opinion in the United States and the Consequences of Muslim Women Stereotypes

In the previous chapter, we discussed public and media stereotypes of Muslim women and how the media can influence these stereotypes. In this chapter, we discuss the stereotypes that are most likely to influence public opinion. While stereotypes assign attributes to groups, public opinion consists of beliefs about the prejudice or differential treatment that Muslim women might encounter in their communities. We also present an argument for the premise that Muslim women are more likely than Muslim men to be victims of aggression and hate crimes.

Studies that explore general stereotypes of Muslims in the media reveal Muslims predominantly portrayed as a threat. To Western societies, Muslims are depicted as terrorists (e.g., Green, 2015; Alsultany, 2012, Farouqui, 2009; El-Aswad, 2013) and barbarians (e.g., Brown, 2006) or a threat to women. Muslims, especially Muslim men, are often portrayed as dominant and repressive toward women (e.g., Abdeslam, 2020). Consistently with the stereotypes of Muslim women, stereotypes of Muslims in general emphasize the differences and incompatibilities of norms, values, and interests of Muslim cultures with Western cultures (e.g., Byng, 2010; Muscati, 2002; Moaddel, 2002).

Such portrayals of Muslims are not new. After the events of 9/11, they became more intensified (e.g., Said, 1978). As with the coverage of Muslim women, media also started extensively focusing on the coverage of Muslim men, but only when they are engaged in acts of violence (Baker, Gabrielatos & McEnery, 2013, p. 253). Such a selective biased coverage of Muslim men thus served the further deterioration of stereotypes of Muslims (e.g., Orbe & Harris, 2013; Issaka, 2021). The construct of Muslim stereotypes got normalized in terms of "global terrorism, Islamic jihadism, fanatic Islamism, fundamentalism, fascism, and Islamic authoritarianism" (El-Aswad, 2013, p. 39).

The generalization of all Muslims as a threat or terrorists turned both Muslim men and women into fearful objects (see Kwan, 2008). However, the effect that such stereotypes have on daily life experiences are stronger for Muslim women than for Muslim men. Such a difference can be explained by the complexity of Muslim women identities (e.g., Perry, 2014). As general stereotypes of Muslims differ from the stereotypes of Muslim women, in this chapter we explore the consequences of media stereotypes on public opinion and Muslim women's daily life experiences.

PUBLIC OPINION AND STEREOTYPES OF MUSLIMS AFTER 9/11

Sides and Gross (2013) concluded that post 9/11 Muslim stereotypes consist of two dimensions: competence (hardworking and intelligent) and warmth (peaceful and trustworthy). American adults perceive Muslims to be competent but not warm. These stereotypes, particularly the warmth dimension, direct evaluations and opinions. For example, respondents who rated Muslims low on the warmth dimension were the most likely to support public policies supporting the War on Terror such as decreased spending on foreign aid, increased spending on border security, and increased spending on the War on Terror (Sides & Gross, 2013).

More recent public opinion polls show shifts in Americans' public opinion toward Muslims. Indeed, attention to Islam and Muslims has grown significantly after the 9/11 attacks (e.g. Panagopoulos, 2006). Americans today acknowledge that Muslims experience a lot of discrimination in American society, an acknowledgment that there is an anti-Muslim bias in the United States (see El-Aswad, 2013). According to a Pew Research Center (2009), there are "modest increases in Americans' familiarity with Islam compared with the months following the 9/11 attacks. Those people who know a Muslim are less likely to see Islam as encouraging of violence; similarly, those who are most familiar with Islam and Muslims are most likely to express favorable views of Muslims and to see similarities between Islam and their own religion" (see also El-Aswad, 2013).

These opinions are based on personal experiences with Muslims which have increased since 9/11 (Ibid). However, in 2014 a Pew Research Center survey reported only 38% of Americans said that they know a Muslim personally (Pew Research Center, 2014; see also Lajevardi, 2021). Also, people who consider Muslims as culturally distinct from the Western mainstream were most likely to maintain negative perceptions of Muslims and Islam (Ciftci, 2012, p. 303). On the political and ideological spectrum, these people are usually conservatives and Republicans (Pew Research

Center, 2017). At the same time, while conservative Americans continue maintaining negative perceptions of Muslims, the same Pew Research Center (2017) study suggests overall warmer perceptions of Muslims by the American audience in comparison to the previous years' Pew Research Center studies.

Although there are studies and survey on public perceptions of Muslims across the world (e.g., Pew Research Center, 2017), there are not that many studies that explore recent American public opinion on Muslims and Muslim Americans (see Lajevardi, 2021). The polls that evaluate public opinion toward Muslim women barely exist.

To conclude, the stereotypes of Muslim women are more complex, mirrors of stereotypes of Muslims in general but including additional dimensions specific to women. Most studies of Muslim women stereotypes have suggested, as in studies of stereotypes of Muslims in general, a binary categorization—of "good" or "evil." On one hand, Muslim women are perceived in the West to be oppressed and powerless, often in need of liberation, and as willing participants in Islamic practices and doctrines that "oppress" (in the eyes of most Westerners) women. On the other hand, Muslim women are perceived to be threats to Western civilization. Unlike the terrorist threats implicit in stereotypes of Muslims in general, Muslim women are seen as cultural threats—they are out of place, their values and beliefs are inconsistent with Western culture, and they accept practices (e.g., male domination) that are not acceptable in Western societies (e.g., Soltani, 2016; Terman, 2017).

Existing studies do not provide information regarding a nuanced evaluation of Muslim women by the public beyond the "bad"/ "good" binary. More dimensions of stereotypes have been found for Muslims in general, but would the same dimensions apply to Muslim women? Recent studies show Muslim women face violence and harassment due to their clothing (Pew Research Center, 2020). These experiences of Muslim women have been linked to the anxiety of the Americans, and more generally—Western, public, partially caused by Muslim women's clothing (e.g., Panagopoulos, 2006; Kalkan et al., 2009). It's unclear whether Muslim women are perceived in other dimensions besides "evil" and "good."

CONSEQUENCES OF PUBLIC OPINION ON MUSLIM WOMEN'S EXPERIENCES

Women, especially Muslim women, experience violence differently than any other minority groups or Muslim men, specifically. Their cultural and religious peculiarities imply that they are more at risk of becoming victims of Islamophobic violence (e.g., Perry, 2014; Mescoli, 2016). Perry (2014) explains that all the general stereotypes of Muslims in US media are equally applied to Muslim women. However, in addition, Muslim women experience the pressure of gender stereotypes which exoticize and sexualize their bodies while simultaneously distinguish them from the Western idea of womanhood. Media stereotypes of Muslim women' experiences are also complicated by class, gender, ethnicity, race, and religion (see Crenshaw, 1990; also, Abu-Ras & Suarez, 2009).

Partially due to media portrayals, women who wear veils are easier to identify as Muslims. As a result, veiled women are more prone to become victims of hate crime and harassment (Zahedi, 2011). Calvo-Barbero & Carrasco-Compos (2020) argue that overall, the image of a Muslim woman is a dominant category that often represents a symbol of religious and patriarchal oppression (see also Valdés-Peña, 2013). These images of Muslim women are perpetuated by the media that continues promoting the fear of Islamophobia (Bayraklı & Hafez, 2017) and further stereotyping Muslim women, especially those who wear veils (Mescoli, 2016).

Overall, the reasons for Islamophobic violence against Muslim women can be both the same and different from the ones that trigger similar violence against Muslim men. For instance, Aziz (2012) explains negative stereotypes can play a role: "Like Muslim males, she too bears the brunt of entrenched stereotypes profiling Muslims as the primary threat to American national security. But unlike her male counterpart, the headscarved Muslim woman is caught at the intersection of discrimination against religion and discrimination against women" (p. 25).

While Bullock and Jafri (2002) examined Muslims' stereotypes with implications to Canadian society, the same arguments can be applied to American society as well. Bullock and Jafri (2002) explain Muslim women are subject to other gender constructs that make them more vulnerable to violence and harassment (see also Jiwani, 2005). Thus, Bullock and Jafri (2002, p. 36; see also Posetti, 2007) show that the stereotypes of Muslim women have stronger societal pressure on what is expected from Muslim women in comparison to Muslim men, what Muslim women "are supposed to be and do" (Nayak, 2006, p. 47, see also Perry, 2014).

To summarize, like most stereotypes in general, American perceptions of Muslim women as oppressed, misogynistic, and without personal agency are not necessarily grounded in reality. For the most part, these perceptions are based on biased portrayals in the media including frequent use of visual symbols (such as clothing) that accentuate differences and reinforce out-group distinctions. Lost in media narratives is the wide variety in values, beliefs, behaviors, and personal accomplishments of Muslim women who are not unlike all other women in their diversity. Soltani (2016) provides an example of this diversity in her analysis of why Muslim women wear a hijab:

> During the European colonial period, for example, the hijab was worn by Muslim women as a sign of anti-colonial resistance to reaffirm their identity and culture. Several studies in the UK and the U.S. also reveal that for some Muslim women, Islamic dress and the veil function as strong statements of identity. For Muslim women living in Europe and the United States, wearing the veil is a way of forming an ethno-religious identity – a way of belonging. (p. 5).

Yet, while Muslim women see the veil as the element of their cultural identity, Western societies have a different perception of Muslim women. In the West, Muslim women's clothing are symbols of an out-group, a threat to native cultures. The female scarf is primarily considered a symbol of religious fundamentalism and patriarchal oppression. Hijabs, veils and burqas, because they provide unusual and unique visual images, can prime implicit stereotypes, evaluations and behaviors toward Muslim women, including the amplification of the Islamophobic violence against them.

While cases of gendered Islamophobia have been receiving more attention in the European countries recently, this subject has not been explored much in the North American context. It is therefore relevant to discuss and explore how negative stereotypes of Muslim women influence public opinion and implications for their interactions in society.

Chapter 4

Priming and Activation Control of Stereotypes

A major premise of this book is that stereotypes of Muslim women are activated by semantic and visual symbols in the environment and that activation in turn can affect evaluations and behaviors toward them. These symbols are primes that activate latent, subconscious mental constructions of groups developed through repetitive and constant exposure to verbal and pictorial representations primarily in childhood. Found in day-to-day interactions and by observation, primes are also found in the media—books, television, advertisements, and social media. The mechanisms by which latent stereotypes are activated to direct related evaluations of and behaviors toward target persons are explained by priming theory.

PRIMING THEORY

According to priming theory, most mental processes governing human perceptions of other people occur outside conscious awareness or control. Traditionally, human perceptual processes and related evaluations and behaviors were attributed to conscious and deliberate thought. However, most of the research on social cognitions in social psychology (albeit not in communication) in the past three decades has been dominated by theories of automacity (e.g., Bargh, Schwader, Hailey, Dyer & Boothby, 2012). According to automacity theories, the development and activation of social-perceptual processes such as impression formation and stereotyping operate outside conscious awareness and control. For example, we are not aware that our stereotypes of other people have been developed through cumulative experiences and exposure to environmental representations, are stored in our subconscious memories, and that they can direct evaluations of and behaviors toward target groups. Most studies of stereotypes using explicit measures show little stereotyping. In some studies, less than 50% of samples admit to explicit stereotypes. On the other hand, studies using implicit measures such as the IAT show extensive stereotyping. Up to 80% of IAT samples reveal implicit stereotyping (e.g., Nosek, Hawkins & Frazier, 2011). These results suggest that most stereotyping is indeed unconscious rather than conscious.

Unconscious stereotypes are based on associations between attributes or traits and groups stored in memory and developed cumulatively from stimuli in the environment. When these associations are repeatedly encountered, the associations and therefore the stereotypes are strengthened although the individual may not be aware that he/she has made those associations.

AUTOMATIC ACTIVATION OF STEREOTYPES AND THEIR APPLICATION

Early theories of automacity conceptualized the activation of stereotypes as a three-step process (e.g., Fiske, 1998; Schneider, 2004—in Muller & Rothermund, 2014). First, the object of the stereotype is placed in a category such as a social group; second, traits associated with the category are activated by primes; and third, evaluations of and behavior toward the individual are directed by the activated traits.

More recently, researchers have distinguished between stereotype activation and stereotype application (e.g., Blair & Banaji, 1996). Stereotype activation is the unconscious assignment of traits (a stereotype) to a group member. Activation is facilitated by primes in the environment such as the mere presence of the "target" person (Bargh et al., 2012) or primes in the media (e.g., Verhaeghen, Aikman, & Van Gulick, 2011). Stereotype activation is a necessary but not sufficient condition for stereotype application. Stereotypes can be activated, but the perceiver may not apply them in evaluations of and actions toward the target person (Blair & Banaji, 1996). Application depends on perceiver intentions and available cognitive resources. Intent is whether the perceiver has the motivation to apply activated stereotypes to the target person. Influenced by cultural norms such as the value placed on equality, intent has to be consciously held for it to prevent the applications of the stereotypes. Intent can be brought to the consciousness or awareness of the perceiver by verbal reminders of the equity norm and by introspection about the perceiver's reasons for believing the activated stereotypes (Blair & Banaji, 1996).

Stereotype activation and application are likely to be unconscious processes when cognitive resources are limited, as when the perceiver reacts to primes in limited time, milliseconds in some studies (Blair & Banaji, 1996), seconds in "shoot and don't shoot scenarios" (Correll et al., 2002).

While the activation of stereotypes is generally an unconscious process, the application of stereotypes can be either conscious or unconscious depending on the available cognitive resources. With enough time to respond to the target person, motivated people will consciously or unconsciously attempt to control application of the activated stereotypes. Therefore, negative stereotypes will not automatically lead to negative evaluations and behaviors.

The distinction between stereotype activation and application has led to a "Quad model" to explain how activated stereotypes might influence applications (Nosek, Hawkins & Frazier, 2011). In this model, four distinct processes contribute to stereotype application: (1) Activation of the stereotype which is usually an automatic, unconscious process; (2) Overcoming the biasing effects of the stereotype to make the correct (non-biased) response, which can be accomplished when cognitive resources are available such as more time; (3) Controlled processing of an unbiased response with motivation to be unbiased and with cognitive resources available; and (4) Guessing at a response when controlled processing does not lead to a defined outcome. The Quad model explains when activated negative stereotypes are not applied. The key processes are controlled processing to overcome biasing effects which is accomplished when cognitive resources such as more time to respond are available to the perceiver, when the perceiver is reminded of social norms, and through introspection. Support for the Quad model is provided in several studies including Gonsalkokorale et al. (2009) who found that the stronger implicit preferences for Whites over Blacks by elderly adults compared to younger adults was explained by greater difficulty in overcoming bias (a failure to inhibit the automatic response) rather than the memory store of negative associations of negative traits with Blacks. The competing explanation not supported by the study was that older adults compared to younger adults were exposed since childhood to more negative portrayals of Blacks in the environment.

SEMANTIC PRIMES

Priming theories start with the basic proposition that impressions of other people including stereotypes are held unconsciously and can be automatically activated when an environmental stimulus is encountered that makes the connections or associations stored in memory. These stimuli can be words or semantic primes (Verhaeghen, Aikman, & Van Gulick, 2011).

Traits can be associated in memory with objects such as groups through repeated pairings of words. Paired words can take on equivalent meanings such that one word becomes synonymous with the other. In stereotyping, one word is often the object of the stereotype, such as a racial category. Other words that can be associated with the object are traits. Examples from recent research using the IAT are Black—violent; Female—caring; Old—slow; Muslim—terrorist (e.g., Nosek et al., 2011). These stereotypical congruent traits are more easily activated compared to stereotypical incongruent words such as Black—rich; Female—strong; Old—fast; Muslim—kind, which are less frequently paired in IAT studies. Semantic priming of stereotypes by words is facilitated by repeated associations of a stereotype object and descriptors in the environment.

Research has shown that names identifying a person in a racial, religious, ethnic, or gender category are powerful primes that activate stereotypes and their application. Job applicants identified by their names as Black, Muslim, an immigrant, or female, activate negative stereotypes and the application of those stereotypes resulting in negative evaluations and rejection (Bertrand & Mullainathan, 2004; Ziegert & Hanges, 2005; Rooth, 2010; Moss-Racusin et al., 2012). Similar results have been found for social interactions. Names associated with racial and ethnic minorities activate negative evaluations of behaviors and intentions in social interactions (McConnell & Liebold, 2001; Gawronski, Geshke, & Banse, 2003.) In these studies, a name activated negative stereotypes which directed evaluations of behavioral intent toward the targeted group.

VISUAL PRIMES

Another model of stereotype priming takes a more general view, stating that any cue in the environment that associates a group with traits can activate latent stereotypes. These cues or primes can be semantic. They can also be visual such as still or moving pictures. For example, repeated viewing in television entertainment or news pairing Blacks with violent crime, weapons, and victims can lead to an unconscious stereotype of Blacks as violent criminals (e.g., Eberhardt et al., 2004). This unconscious stereotype can be activated by cues in the environment such as a weapon or the presence of a Black man in a crime scene. Associative co-occurrences of visual primes and stereotyped groups are powerful activators of implicit stereotypes (e.g., Verhaeghen et al., 2011). Studies have shown that a photograph of a Black man can activate stereotypes of Blacks as criminals, resulting in misidentification of crime suspects, biased evaluation of evidence in a courtroom, and greater willingness "to shoot" and reluctance to "not shoot" (Oliver & Fonash, 2002; Levinson & Young, 2010; Rachilinski et al., 2009; Correll et al., 2014). Similar to results of studies of Blacks in the shooter bias paradigm, photos of Muslim men in headgear activated stereotypes of Muslims as terrorists, resulting in a bias to shoot more frequently and in less time compared to non-Muslim men (Unkelbach et al., 2008).

MEDIA PRIMES

The influence of media primes—verbal and visual symbols in television, newspapers, advertisements, and social media—is reactive. The perceiver does not intentionally seek out media contents with these cues which can be present in his/her everyday consumption of news and entertainment. Cumulatively, these symbols develop and reinforce negative stereotypes of out-groups. Individually, a symbol can activate stereotypes. Media primes can be verbal, as in headlines associating Muslims with terrorism, or visual, such as a photograph or television shot showing a Muslim woman in burqa holding a gun. Although there have been more balanced portrayals of racial minorities in American media in the past decade (Mastro, 2009), most portrayals are negative, as in the association of young Black men with violent crime (e.g., Eberhardt et al., 2004.) Balanced portrayals of Muslims and Muslim women are rare; most portrayals are negative. (See Chapters 2 and 3 of this book). Professional journalists' organizations such as the Asian American Journalists Association, the National Association of Black Journalists, and the National Association of Hispanic Journalists have called for more balanced portrayals, much in the same way that White majorities are portrayed (e.g., Asian American Journalists Association, 2020). Imbalanced portrayals, such as frequent associations of Blacks with crime, can disproportionately affect implicit stereotypes even when neutralized with positive associations such as a young Black man accepting a college scholarship. Research on the emotions of implicit stereotyping shows that negative emotions and negative portrayals are more influential than positive emotions and positive portrayals in the development of implicit stereotypes (Tan, 2021).

A meta-analysis of media priming effects has shown that these effects are consistent and reliable (Roskos-Ewoldson, Klinger, & Roskos-Ewoldson, 2007; Ramasubramanian, 2007). Media primes produce and reproduce (activate) stereotypes. These effects have been observed for both verbal and visual primes, with repeated exposure and a single exposure (e.g., Mastro, 2009; Abraham & Appiah, 2006).

ACTIVATION CONTROL

Although implicit stereotypes can be activated by primes with repeated or single exposures, activation can be controlled under certain conditions (Blair & Banaji, 1996; Arendt, 2013). Research has identified the following conditions:

Motivation

Perceivers can be motivated to avoid stereotyping by making them aware that an opportunity for stereotyping exists—that is, the opportunity to subconsciously or consciously assign traits to a social group such as a racial minority. This awareness can be brought about by asking the perceiver to describe a group from a list of traits (conscious or explicit stereotypes) or by pairing group cues such as a photograph or a name with positive or negative traits. The pairing of group identifiers with traits signals to most people that stereotyping can occur, an awareness that can block stereotyping.

Most motivations require some degree of awareness that generalizing traits to an entire group is stereotyping. The motivation to avoid stereotyping arises from a perceiver's intentions not to be biased and to treat everyone equally, a product of socialization in which self-concepts and values are established. Stereotyping is blocked when the intention to be egalitarian is primed by messages and symbols in the environment such as media appeals to be fair and to treat everyone equally.

Motives may be self-serving, such as to preserve and protect a self-image (Blair, 2002). Studies have shown that self-image threat, such as when a negative stereotype of the self is activated, as when given bogus information that one has scored poorly in an intelligence test, can motivate people to invoke negative stereotypes of others (Spencer et al., 1977). Evaluating others negatively by assigning undesirable traits to them helps to restore a positive self-image.

Motives can be social, influenced by perceived group norms and expectations (Blair, 2002). For example, negative stereotyping of racial minorities by extremist hate groups such as White supremacists is facilitated by perceived in-group consensus in social media (Gardner, 2018). Conversely, most people will refrain from stereotyping when reminded of the egalitarian values of the community.

Restricted Cognitive Resources

Allport (1954) referred to stereotyping as a cognitively lazy process. Stereotypes are convenient, efficient although often erroneous heuristics for the evaluation of people. They are most likely activated when cognitive resources of the perceiver are limited (Blair & Banaji, 1996). Cognitive processes can be limited by the pressures of time such as milliseconds in which to make a judgment as in the IAT, seconds to make a decision to "shoot or don't shoot" (Nosek et al., 2011; Correll et al., 2014). A general principle is that the less time to respond to a stereotype object, the more likely implicit and explicit stereotypes will be activated (Blair & Banaji, 1996).

Rigid information processing can also limit cognitive resources that control stereotyping. Numerous studies comparing the information processing strategies of members of extremist hate groups show that they, compared to nonmembers, prefer simple answers such as "Yes" or "No" to complicated questions (Schaffner, 2018). A longitudinal study in the United Kingdom showed that young adults who revealed prejudicial attitudes in explicit and implicit tests had scored lower on traditional tests of intelligence when they were children, controlling for income and education. However, this correlation decreased when social conservatism in adulthood was controlled, leading the researchers to conclude that "less intelligent" children grow up to be social conservatives who are more likely to be racists than nonconservatives (Hodson & Busseri, 2010).

There is general agreement among researchers that limited cognitive resources lead to a greater probability of stereotype activation. This is particularly evident for stereotype applications (Blair & Banaji, 1996) which typically require more cognitive effort for the correct response (unbiased evaluations and behaviors) and therefore more time. When time and cognitive resources are restricted, the association between the activated stereotype and its application becomes "automatic," less under the control of the receiver.

Dose

Dose of the environmental prime associating an out-group with negative stereotypical traits can control the activation of implicit and negative stereotypes. Also called frequency, length and intensity of group-trait associations, doses control activation of stereotypes by first, making the perceiver aware that a stereotyping situation exists, and second, by activating motivations to block stereotyping. High prime doses can lead to activation control of stereotypes (e.g., Arendt, 2013.) In one study, eight repetitions of the association between crime and immigrants in news stories led to less negative explicit stereotyping compared to moderate and low repetitions (Arendt, 2013). Perceivers consciously or unconsciously recognized that the high doses were "blatant" attempts at providing a one-sided negative picture of the out-group, recognition which motivated them to avoid stereotypes.

COUNTERING STEREOTYPE ACTIVATION

When the perceiver is motivated to control negative stereotypes and when cognitive resources are not restricted, the activation of negative stereotypes and their application can be prevented (Blair, 2002). Some of the strategies to counter stereotype activation are initiated by the perceiver, while others are directed by external cues such as primes in the media. We discuss these strategies as they apply to Muslim women in more detail in chapter 7 (Interventions Applied to Muslim Women). In this section, we discuss general strategies as they apply to priming and stereotype activation:

- Suppression: perceivers are instructed to "reduce their stereotyping," and to judge others in a fair and unbiased way.
- Promotion of counter stereotypes. Exemplars, or representative examples of the targeted group, can neutralize negative stereotypes by emphasizing positive traits. Positive exemplars lead to liking, which prevents negative stereotyping. The most effective antidote to negative stereotyping is the paring of positive exemplars of the targeted group (e.g., Black Americans) with negative exemplars of the majority group (e.g., White Americans). Negative exemplars of the majority group provide perceivers a baseline of comparison with positive exemplars of the targeted group, resulting in the activation of positive traits for the targeted group (Dasgupta & Greenwald, 2001).
- Focus of attention, social cues, and the configuration of primes. Stereotypes can dominate the evaluation of individuals unless the perceiver spends more time learning about the target person's unique attributes. When the perceiver uses the easy or "lazy" heuristic, then the evaluation is based on stereotypes. Since many of these evaluations occur under constraints of time, effort and ability, the context in which primes is encountered can influence which stereotypes are activated. Context defines which group category of the target person is the most relevant to the present situation calling for an evaluation (e.g., for a job applicant, gender, religion, or race). Physical appearance (e.g., skin tone), attire (e.g., hijab or burqa) and environment (e.g., target person in a bombed-out building or in a hospital) are examples of context. Studies show that context provides powerful primes that determine which stereotypes are activated. Macrae et al. (1995) showed research participants photos of a Chinese woman either putting on make-up or using chopsticks, then measured automatic stereotypes of both Chinese and women. Compared to a control group, participants who saw the woman putting on make-up were faster to respond to trait stereotypes of women and slower to respond to trait stereotypes of Chinese. Participant who saw the woman using chopsticks were faster to respond to Chinese stereotypical traits and were slower to respond to stereotypical traits of women. Wittenbrink, Judd and Park (2001) showed research participants a video of Black Americans at an outdoor barbecue or a video of Black Americans in a gang-related setting. The barbecue video led to more negativity toward Blacks as measured by the IAT compared to the gang-related video. Livingston and Brewer (2002) found that Black Americans in photos with "more Negroid"

characteristics elicited more automatic prejudices than Black Americans in photos with "less Negroid" characteristics.

These studies provide evidence that the context in which primes are presented can influence the contents of stereotypes activated. Context prevents the activation of negative stereotypes by directing attention to another group associated with the target person.

A PRIMING MODEL OF THE ACTIVATION AND APPLICATION OF UNCONSCIOUS STEREOTYPES

A model which summarizes the process by which primes activate implicit or unconscious stereotypes is shown in figure 4.1. The process begins in early childhood as developmental inputs which lead to associative memory linking objects and attributes. These linkages, although subconsciously held (the individual is not aware that he/she has made them) influence responsiveness of the individual to verbal and semantic symbols or primes that reinforce them. Primes, whether intentionally or accidentally exposed to, activate object-attribute linkages as stereotypes. Activation control of stereotypes and their application can be accomplished by individual and informational strategies.

DEVELOPMENTAL INPUTS

Early Experiences

Unconscious or implicit stereotypes have their origins in past and largely forgotten experiences (Rudman, 2004). Beginning in pre-verbal childhood, these experiences provide the basis for trait-target group associations, teaching the child indirectly affective connections between other people and self.

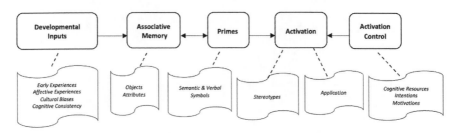

Figure 4.1 A Priming Model of the Activation and Application of Unconscious Stereotypes. *Source*: Created by authors.

These associations are learned by observation and provide a foundation for later learning. For example, pre-verbal attachment to maternal caregivers is associated with liking for women in general (Rudman, 2004). Similar associations have been found for race. Early liking for a particular person can be generalized to liking for that person's observed group category. Later in life, pleasant experiences translate into positive automatic stereotypes of people sharing in or responsible for those experiences, particularly when repeated. These experiences can be direct, person-to-person, or vicarious as observed in television, movies, or as related by peers. Media contents that elicit positive emotions toward an out-group can have similar effects on implicit stereotypes as direct experiences (Bandura, 1986).

Affective Experiences

Implicit stereotypes are based on associations between traits and groups that arouse emotions even when presented to the perceiver in limited time (Rudman, Ashmore, & Gary, 2001). Repeated negative associations as, for example, between crime and Blacks lead to negative stereotypes that become imbedded in the perceiver's subconscious network of trait- group attributions. When primed with cues, these subconscious associations are activated as stereotypes that can influence evaluations and behavior. Implicit stereotypes originate from automatic emotional responses to associations, while explicit stereotypes (those that the perceiver is consciously aware of) are based on cognitively controlled processes (Rudman et al., 2001).

Cultural Biases

The perceiver's social environment or culture influences the development of implicit stereotypes beginning with pre-verbal children (Rudman, 2004). Children as young as six months recognize physical group differences such as skin color and gender (Katz, 2003). The ability to categorize objects and people develop into the ability to make positive or negative evaluations, stored networks of traits and groups or stereotypes. As children are exposed to portrayals of groups in the media, the potential for influence by observed associations, no matter how briefly, is significantly increased. Society's views of groups are portrayed and reinforced in the environment including the media. These views are summarized by trait-group associations or stereotypes. They are internalized, stored in subconscious memory, and activated when cued by primes.

Cognitive Consistency

People prefer consonant or consistent evaluations of related attitude objects to dissonant or inconsistent evaluations (Festinger, 1978). Consistency is achieved when a stereotype, for example, is consistent with the perceiver's self-concept as an unbiased person. Learned early in life from significant others (parents, teachers), these self-concepts cumulatively influence the trait-group associations in the environment that a perceiver will store. A person who has developed a self-concept as an unbiased person will less likely have a store of negative trait-group associations compared to a person who does not have an unbiased self-concept and will be less likely to have a store of negative stereotypes.

ASSOCIATIVE MEMORY

Developmental inputs are stored in memory as mental associations between words, pictures, and experiences linking attributes and emotions to groups. Repetition of these associations strengthens the link; the stronger the link, the more accessible and available the associations are for activation as stereotypes. The process by which these associations are stored is largely unconscious. The perceiver is not aware that he or she is making the associations which are stored in long-term memory (Blair & Banaji, 1996; Arendt, 2013.) For example, babies who are cared for by nurturing women (a pleasant experience) will store a memory linking women with liking and pleasure. Children who repeatedly watch television entertainment featuring Black Americans as gang members and violent criminals will store a memory of Blacks as violent and criminal.

PRIMES

The associations between groups, traits, and emotions from developmental inputs are largely dormant. They do not exist in memory as stereotypes. However, primes or cues in the environment can activate stored associations as stereotypes. Activation is largely unconscious—the perceiver is not aware that he/she has associated a trait with a group (Bargh et al., 2012; Nosek et al., 2011).

As noted earlier in this chapter, primes can be verbal or visual. Examples of verbal primes are in news report headlines and stories are "thugs," "terrorists," "rapists," "murderers," "socialists." Examples of visual primes are a cartoon depiction of a chimpanzee; a wet market in China; a Muslim woman wearing hijab; or simply a member of the targeted group. These words and visuals can activate previously stored associations, particularly when simultaneously paired with a related concept stored in memory—Blacks with violence, immigrants with criminals, Asians with the COVID 19 virus.

ACTIVATION OF STEREOTYPES
AND THEIR APPLICATIONS

Unconscious associations activated by primes as stereotypes are not necessarily applied by the perceiver. Blair and Banaji (1996) have shown that stereotype activation is an automatic process that operates when appropriate situational cues or primes are present, while stereotype application can be controlled. Stereotype activation is less likely to be controllable than stereotype application which can be controlled by increasing cognitive resources and by activating motivations to be unbiased (discussed in a previous section of this chapter).

Research has confirmed that activated subconscious stereotypes influence evaluations and behaviors, but that these applications can also be controlled (e.g., Tan, 2021). Among the applications of activated subconscious stereotypes are:

- Hiring Evaluations and Practices (Bertrand & Mullainathan, 2004; Ziegert & Hanges, 2005; Rooth, 2010; Moss-Racusin et al., 2012).
- Political Attitudes and Behaviors (Greenwald, Smith et al., 2009; Knowles, Lowery & Schaumberg, 2010; Hodson & Busseri, 2010; Stephan & Stephan, 2000; Luttig et al., 2017; Schaffner, 2018).
- Health Care Disparities (De Angelis, 2019; Ponner et al., 2010; Green et al., 2007).
- Social Interactions (McConnell & Leibold, 2001; Gawronski, Geshke, & Banse, 2003).
- Evaluating Evidence in the Courtroom (Levinson & Young, 2010; Rachlinski et al., 2009; Ayres & Waldfogel, 1994; Mustard, 2001; Levinson, Cal & Young, 2010; Bielen, Marneffe, & Mocan, 2018).
- Racial Profiling (Satzewich & Shaffir, 2009; Persico, 2008; Pittman, 2020; Stanford Open Policing Project, 2020; Starr, 2016).
- Identification and Misidentification of Criminal Suspects (Oliver & Fonash, 2002).
- Shooter bias: "Shoot or Don't Shoot" (Correll, Park, Judd & Wittenbrink, 2007; Correll et al., 2011; Correll et al., 2014).
- Ageism: (Lyons, 2009; Cuddy et al., 2005; Happell, 2002; Barnes et al., 2006; O'Keefe et al., 2007).

In these studies, negative explicit and implicit stereotypes led to negative evaluations of and behaviors toward the target group (see Tan (2021) for a discussion of the studies). Implicit stereotypes as measured by the IAT were stronger predictors of the stereotype applications, compared to explicit stereotypes.

ACTIVATION CONTROL

The activation of stereotype applications is more responsive to control strategies than the activation of stereotypes themselves. Stereotypes are activated when the perceiver assigns attributes to a group. This process may be largely unconscious. Stereotype applications are activated when the perceiver uses the stereotypes to direct evaluations of and behaviors toward a group. This process, although based on stereotypes that may be unconsciously held, allows the perceiver to pause and reflect on his/her use of the stereotype and is therefore more amenable to control. Control of stereotype applications can be accomplished by training, by reinforcing motivations to be equitable, and by using informational strategies such as exemplars to counter stereotypes (discussed in an earlier section of this chapter and in chapter 7, Interventions Applied to Muslim Women).

APPLICATION OF THE PRIMING
MODEL TO MUSLIM WOMEN

This book is guided by the priming model of stereotype activation and application (figure 4.1). We apply the model to stereotypes of Muslim women in the United States. We provide supporting evidence for each component of the model in these chapters:

- Developmental Inputs: Chapter 2 (Historical and Current Stereotypes of Muslim Women in the United States and the Role of the Media in Their Formation).
- Cognitive Associations; Subconscious and Conscious Stereotypes: Chapter 5 (Priming Negative Stereotypes of Muslim Women: Antecedents and Consequences).
- Primes: Chapter 6 (Semantic and Visual Primes of Stereotypes of Muslim Women: Activation and Activation Control).
- Stereotype Activation and Application: Chapter 5 (Priming Negative Stereotypes of Muslim Women: Antecedents and Consequences).
- Activation Control: Chapter 7: Interventions Applied to Muslim Women.

In the next chapter, we discuss how negative stereotypes of Muslim women are activated and consequences of activation.

Chapter 5

Priming Negative Stereotypes of Muslim Women

Antecedents and Consequences

When placed in a category, Muslim women are convenient targets of prejudice and negative stereotyping because "Muslim woman" has multiple layers of identification, each layer with its own set of negative stereotypes commonly accepted in Western cultures. Islam is often associated with terrorism and violence in the United States, particularly after 9/11 and during the Trump administration (Pew Research Center, 2017, Ciftci, 2012). For example, almost half of Americans believe Muslims in the US are anti-American (Pew Research Center, 2019, 2017). Islam is often misunderstood and feared in the West. The Runnymode Trust (2017) identified eight components of Islamophobia: (1) Islam is a monolithic block, static and unresponsive to change; (2) Islam is separate from the West and the "other"; (3) Islam is "inferior to the west, barbaric, irrational, primitive and sexist"; (4) Islam is "violent, aggressive, threatening and supporting of terrorism"; (5) Islam is a political ideology that is "used for political or military advantage."

MUSLIM WOMEN ARE EASY STEREOTYPE TARGETS

Although religion may be the most influential, gender and ethnicity also contribute to negative stereotyping of Muslim women. Women in general are stereotyped as compassionate, warm, indecisive, emotional, and more suited for the home than for careers as leaders in business or politics (Pew Research Center, 2008; Moss-Racusin et al., 2012). Arabs are "backward," cruel, fanatics, and resistant to change (Shaheen, 2008; Sides & Gross, 2013). Taken together, these characterizations based on religion, gender, and ethnicity are easily and conveniently assigned to Muslim women when personal contact is lacking and when reinforced by the media. This is particularly true in the United States and other Western countries. About 70% of adults in the European Union say they know "very little" about Islam, and their main source of information about Islam is the media (Johnson, 2019). Similar percentages have been reported for the United States (Pew Research Center, 2017; Johnson, 2019). Muslim women carry the additional burden, compared to Muslim men, of gender and ethnic stereotypes (discussed in more detail in chapter 2 of this book).

FASHION AS A STEREOTYPE PRIME OF MUSLIM WOMEN

In addition to physical features, Muslim women are visible primes for stereotyping when they wear fashion that signals their identities. Fashion associated with Islam includes the hijab (a veil that covers the hair and head but leaves the face uncovered), the niqab (face veil that covers the whole face leaving the area around the eyes uncovered), and the burqa (female garment covering the whole body often leaving just a mesh screen for eyes). Because most Westerners are unfamiliar with these fashions, they are often wrongfully perceived to reinforce biases toward Muslims.

Women's Perspectives

The most common Western perception is that Muslim women's fashions are symbols of fundamentalist Islam. They are symbols of oppression and subservience, reinforcing perceptions of the "other" versus "us," the other—Muslims—being threats to Western democratic values (Soltani, 2016). Because these fashions are visible signs, Muslim women are readily identified to be fundamentalist Muslims. Negative stereotypes of Muslims are assigned to women including support of terrorism. In addition, Muslim women are stereotyped to be subservient, oppressed, unable to exercise free choice, passive, need to be enlightened and rescued and victims of patriarchal Muslim societies (Soltani, 2016).

Perspectives of Muslim Women

The perspectives of Muslim women on fashion are more nuanced and varied than Western perspectives. For example, Muslim women say they wear veils for a variety of reasons, many of them personal (Janson, 2011). Although the veil is required of women in some Muslim countries such as Saudi Arabia,

Iran and Afghanistan, many Muslim women say that wearing the veil is a personal decision, a means of expressing self-identity, devotion to Islam, and modesty.

When worn to express identity as a Muslim woman, the veil in some countries such as Egypt is considered by Muslim women as "a voluntary act by women who are deeply committed to being moral and have a sense of honour tied to family" (Abu-Lughod, p. 2002, p. 786). Women choose when and for whom they veil and for whom they do not (Abu-Lughod, 2002). Rather than a symbol of oppression, the veil to many Muslim women is a symbol of their self-identities rooted in family, religion, and culture.

As a religious symbol, the veil is worn by women to express piousness and devotion to Islam rather than to a political cause or action associated by many Westerners with Islam, such as terrorism to spread the religion. Similar to many Catholics wearing the crucifix as a pendant to express their faith, Muslim women wear the veil to express devotion to Islam as a personal choice.

As an expression of modesty, the veil and burqa are based on cultural norms of how women manage their physical interactions with men. Many Muslim women say that they wear the veil to discourage unwanted advances from men. Others say that they choose when and for whom they wear a veil and that their attire in public is different from attire at home. Public modesty is a valued cultural value internalized by many Muslim women and demonstrated in their choice of fashion. Rather than a symbol of oppression, when taken in this context, the veil is a symbol of cultural values and in most Muslim countries—freedom of choice. The double standard in Western perceptions of Muslim women's fashion and Western women's dress is pointed out by Abu-Lughod (2002):

> The veil . . . is the symbol of oppression of a sex. Putting on torn jeans, wearing yellow, green or blue hair, this is an act of freedom with regard to social conventions. Putting a veil in the head, this is an act of submission. (cited in Hirschkind & Mahmoud, 2002, p. 352).

The perspectives of Muslim women on wearing the veil and other fashions show a contrast with Western perceptions. Muslim women's fashions have been politicized in many Western countries. These fashions are symbols of oppression, justifying an ideology that supports the "liberation" of Muslim women from patriarchal Islamic regimes. To most Muslim women, fashion is a choice that they take pride in, and, as in some debates in Western countries (e.g., abortion), a choice that is based on the principle that they have a right to regulate control of their bodies.

PRIMING STEREOTYPES OF MUSLIM WOMEN
IN NEWS AND ENTERTAINMENT

Imagery in news and entertainment media are primary sources of nascent negative perceptions of Muslims and Muslim women and are also primes that activate implicit stereotypes. Images of Muslims as evil and warlike, savage leaders, deceitful, sexually depraved, fanatics, deceitful and manipulative are common in Western television and film (see chapter 2). Muslim women are often shown in situations that activate and reinforce negative gender-based stereotypes, therefore exacerbating the effect of negative portrayals of Muslims in general.

SEMANTIC PRIMES OF ISLAM AND
MUSLIM WOMEN IN THE MEDIA

Words, particularly from leaders, can be powerful activators of implicit biases toward Muslims in general and Muslim women in particular. According to one analysis (Bridge Initiative Team, June 23, 2017), the Trump campaigns and later his administration attempted to gain support by using tailored messages that capitalized on fear, misunderstanding, and negative feelings toward Muslims. These messages revolved around tying Islam to violence and terrorism, making Islam and Muslims the enemy, and not differentiating between "radical extremists" and mainstream Muslims as previous presidents had done. Indicative of this rhetoric were public statements such as:

> "thousands of Muslims were cheering at the collapse of the World Trade Center",
> and referring to Muslims or Islam as "radicals", a political ideology that is a "threat
> to America", "radical Islamic terror," "Islamic fascism", "Muslim rape culture,"
> "Jihad", "Sharia", "a ticking time bomb", "a cancer" that is "metastasizing", at
> "war with America" (Bridge Initiative Team, 2017; Walters & Mouthktar, 2019).

These inflammatory words reinforced and activated latent negative feelings and stereotypes of Muslims and carried over to perceptions of Muslim women. Reference to Muslim women as "oppressed," "fundamentalist," accomplices of terrorists and "brainwashed" contributed to and activated implicit negative perceptions, resulting in discriminatory practices and behaviors such as hate crimes.

EXPLAINING PREJUDICE TOWARD MUSLIM WOMEN:
WHO IS MOST LIKELY TO BE PREJUDICED?

About half of Americans believe that Muslims in the United States are anti-American and large majorities close to 70% believe in negative stereotypes of Muslims (Pew Research Center, 2017). Although these percentages are based on explicit questions in surveys and should therefore be considered explicit stereotypes, they do not necessarily predict evaluations and overt discriminatory actions toward Muslims. More predictable is the link between implicit biases and evaluations and actions toward targeted groups (Nosek et al., 2011). When primed, implicit prejudices lead to negative evaluations and social interactions and in the extreme, aggression and hate crimes. In the following discussion, we identify precursors or antecedents of implicit biases toward Muslim women and their consequences.

GENERALIZED BIAS TOWARD RACIAL MINORITIES

Prejudice against racial minorities and Muslims in general are reliable predictors of prejudice against Muslim women (Johnson, 2019). This generalized antipathy is an important antecedent of anti-Muslim women bias. In the United States and Europe, prejudice directed at racial and ethnic minorities including Muslims has been studied at three levels of analysis.

Individual level: At the individual level, cognitive style, or how people process information, distinguishes prejudiced from less prejudiced individuals. Intolerance of ambiguity and a preference for simple answers are positively related to prejudice: the more intolerance for ambiguity and a greater preference for simplicity, the more prejudiced the individual will be (Jost et al., 2003). Cognitive rigidity, a related concept, predicts resistance to change and a preference for the status quo (Stankov, 2009) which in turn predict prejudice. Cognitive rigidity is defined as a preference for "Yes" or "No" answers, less cognitive flexibility, less openness to alternative perspectives, and less ability to process complex information (Stankov, 2009).

Research consistently shows that people who are prejudiced toward racial minorities, Muslims and Muslim women included, compared to less prejudiced individuals, have lesser capabilities to process complex and new information, particularly information that challenges the status quo. Education reliably predicts a more open cognitive style and less prejudice. General intelligence as measured by standardized tests also predicts a cognitive style that is open to and capable of processing complex information. However, intelligence does not directly predict prejudice. A longitudinal study over 20 years in the United Kingdom showed that intelligence in children 10 and 11 years did not directly predict prejudice in adulthood when social conservatism in adulthood was controlled (Hodson & Busseri, 2012).

Social conservatism was defined as resistance to change and cognitive rigidity. Intelligence in children predicted social conservatism in adulthood. However, the link between intelligence and prejudice was not significant when social conservatism was accounted for, leading to the conclusion that the influence of intelligence on prejudice is indirect. Children who score lower on intelligence tests grow up to be more socially conservative than children who score higher; socially conservative adults are more likely to be prejudiced than adults who are not socially conservative. Therefore, there is no direct link between intelligence and prejudice toward racial minorities, Muslims, or Muslim women. The key predictor is social conservatism. (In chapter 6, we analyze the effects of political ideology, a concept related to social conservatism, on priming of stereotypes of Muslim women).

Also at the individual level, researchers have analyzed the personality profiles of prejudiced individuals. The premise is that people who are prejudiced toward one out-group will also be prejudiced toward other out-groups. Among the personality traits associated with prejudice in general are authoritarianism, social dominance, and paranoia (Pettigrew, 2017). Authoritarianism is characterized by deference to authority and a rigid hierarchical view of the world. Social dominance is characterized by a desire for in-groups to control out-groups, and to assign lower status to out-groups. And paranoia is chronic mistrust and suspicion of others without adequate reason. The combination of these traits defines a racist individual who most likely will be prejudiced against Muslims and Muslim women. Research has shown that authoritarianism and social dominance are related to social conservatism; that these traits singly and in combination predict generalized racism; and that paranoia is correlated with mistrust of Muslims and Islamophobia (e.g., Pettigrew, 2017).

Group level: Group identity predicts hostility or prejudice toward perceived outsiders. When racial and ethnic minorities are perceived to be outsiders, they become available targets for negative stereotyping and related hostile evaluations and acts. Membership in groups facilitates the development of positive self-concepts, primarily when the group reinforces an individual's self-worth. Studies have shown that a primary reason for membership in extremist hate groups such as White supremacists is reinforcement of values and beliefs that support members and devalue non-members (Tan, 2021). The distinction between in-groups and out-groups and the dynamics leading to prejudice against out-groups are foundations of research on racism (e.g., Tajfel, 1979). In the case of Muslim women, labeling and portraying them as an out-group because of religion, gender, ethnicity, and immigration status make them convenient targets for anti-Muslim women prejudice.

Adding to the stigma of an out-group label, racial and other minorities are often perceived to be threats to the mainstream because they are new and "don't fit in." Threats can be symbolic as, for example, perceptions that a group will not integrate into the community and will not adapt the values, language, and culture of the mainstream. Or threats can be realistic, as when minorities are perceived by the mainstream to take away jobs, increase the crime rate, dilute the identity of the mainstream eventually leading to its dissolution (e.g., Stephan & Stephan, 2000). Evidence indicates that perceived realistic and symbolic threats are indeed significant predictors of anti-immigrant prejudice in the United States (Stephan & Stephan, 2000.) Similar results for Muslims have been found in the European Union and the United States (Ciftci, 2012). Attitudes toward Muslims were more negative when they were perceived to be symbolic and realistic threats to the home country of survey respondents.

Threat theory explains why Muslim women are targets of prejudice. Muslim women are perceived in many Western countries to be threats to the cultures of mainstream societies because their values (e.g., perceived acceptance of patriarchal norms) and behaviors (e.g., fashion and perceived lack of agency) are different from norms in Western societies. Combined with perceived realistic threats (e.g., support of "terrorism"), these symbolic threats lead to negative evaluations and actions such as hate crimes directed at Muslim women.

Social level: At the social level, prejudice toward minorities is explained by the cumulative effect of symbols and messages encountered in childhood and throughout the life span that dehumanize and cast minorities as inferior. These symbols and messages, conveyed by socialization agents such as parents, peers, and teachers are reinforced by the media (chapter 2). People develop negative attitudes and stereotypes from this exposure, stored in long-term memory and activated by primes. Stereotypical portrayals of Muslim women as without agency and as willing accomplices in terrorist acts lead to stored negative attitudes and stereotypes which when activated trigger negative actions such as hate crimes.

Analyses of prejudice at the individual, group, and social levels share three principles. First, prejudice is based on the fear of the unknown; Second, to conquer this fear, a person has to be open to new information and third, new information is not easy to find in most societies because information confirming the culture of the mainstream is the dominant narrative in the media and interpersonal communication. Muslim women are perceived by majorities in Western societies to be "different" because of their attire. They are seen as threats because they are different. These perceptions are often based on erroneous and scant information. Neutralizing information—as what may be found in the media—is scarce. Therefore, they are convenient targets for prejudice; implicit biases are easily and frequently primed by symbols in the environment.

MUSLIM WOMEN'S PERCEPTIONS OF
PREJUDICE IN THE UNITED STATES

Muslim women have a more negative view compared to Muslim men about their place in Western nations, the extent of prejudice and discrimination toward Muslims in general, and about media coverage in news and entertainment.

A random sample of adult Muslim men and women living in the United States in 2017 by the Pew Research Center showed that more Muslim women (57%) than men say that it has become more difficult to be Muslim in recent years (Pew Research Center, 2017). More Muslim women than men say that there is a lot of discrimination against Muslims (83% of Muslim women, 68% of Muslim men); that they have been the targets of prejudice such as treated with suspicion, called offensive names, singled out by airport security or other law enforcement, physically threatened or attacked at least once in the past year (55% of Muslim women, 42% of Muslim men); that they stand out in American society because of their appearance, voice, or clothing that distinctively identifies them as Muslim (49% of Muslim women, 27% of Muslim men; and that media coverage of Muslims is unfair and biased (68% of Muslim women, 52% of Muslim men) (Pew Research Center, 2017). Even with these negative views about their place in American society, most Muslim men and women in the United States see a path for a better life for themselves and their families (Pew Research Center, 2017).

These negative perceptions of prejudice against Muslims are more common in large than small cities (Pew, 2017). In-depth interviews with a small sample (N=13) of Muslim women in a small college town where they were either students or were accompanying their husbands who were students reveal more positive perceptions and experiences (Walters & Mouhktar, 2019). The women admitted to some fear and anxiety about moving to the United States because they initially perceived the US as non-welcoming to Arabs and Muslims. This perception was formed from US feature films and news in their home countries that portrayed Muslims as terrorists and enemies of Americans. One respondent referred to the "alarmist imagery," particularly in news, saying "I know they (Americans) fear Muslims" because Muslims are terrorists (Walters & Mouhktar, 2019). These perceptions of unwelcoming Americans are reinforced by family members and participants in online platforms who advise Muslim women not to go to the United States, particularly if they are wearing a hijab (Walters & Mouhktar, 2019). Prior to and soon after relocating to the United States, Muslim women in this study were apprehensive and preparing for the worst. Their experiences, however, in the small college town were very positive. The Muslim women reported that the majority of their American neighbors, friends, and coworkers were helpful and welcoming. These positive experiences can be explained by location in a college town where students and academics are presumably more open about "outsiders" including Muslims, in contrast to a general population where most people, as indicated in national surveys, have negative views of out-groups (Pew Research Center, 2017).

MUSLIM WOMEN AS VICTIMS OF HATE

Negative stereotypes and images of Muslim women have made them convenient and easily identifiable targets for racist anti-Muslim acts including harassment, profiling, verbal abuse, physical intimidation, threats, and attempted or actual physical assault. Although much of the attention and anti-Muslim hate acts after the terrorist acts of 9/11 have focused on Muslim men, Muslim women have been more frequently targeted than Muslim men in many Western countries including Germany, the United Kingdom, France, Belgium, the Netherlands, Canada, and the United States (Perry, 2014). In the United States, Arab and Muslim women experience twice the rate of hate incidents as male Arabs and Muslims (Cainkar, 2009). In a national probability survey of Muslims in the United States, over half of Muslim women (55%) said they had experienced at least one anti-Muslim incident in the past year compared to 42% of Muslim men. In the Netherlands, 90% of complaints of anti-Muslim behaviors were from Muslim victims who were women. Anti-Muslim aggression against Muslim women happens most frequently in public spaces such as public transport, streets, markets, shops, gyms, parks, shopping malls, and the workplace. Hate acts included verbal abuse (" terrorist," "suicide bomber," "letterbox," "Darth Vader," "Ninja," "walking coffin"); and physical abuse such as taking the veil or hijab off, being spat on, shoving, pushing, passing vehicles attempting to run them over; people on the street or moving vehicles throwing eggs, stones, alcohol, water bombs, bottles, takeaway food, and garbage (Zempi, 2016).

Some of the abusive comments reported by victims were misogynistic ("Muslim bitch," Muslim whore," "f. . . freak") (Zempi, 2016). Victims also reported sexual harassment by aggressors such as sexual comments, wolf whistling, catcalling, and sexist jokes (Zempi, 2016). These anti-Muslim acts have been reported in the United States and several European countries including Belgium, Denmark, France, the Netherlands, and the United Kingdom. In these countries, veiled Muslim women and Muslim women wearing the hijab were almost always the victims. In many European countries, over 90% of victims were identifiable as Muslim because they were wearing the hijab or the niqab (Soltani, 2016; Seta, 2016). In the United

States, six in ten Muslim men and women whose appearance identified them as Muslim have experienced hate acts compared to 38% who were not easily identifiable (Pew Research Center, 2017).

INSTITUTIONAL, IDEOLOGICAL, AND PRIMING BASES FOR VICTIMIZATION OF MUSLIM WOMEN

The victimization of Muslim women is grounded on institutional and ideological "othering" of Muslims in general since the terrorist attacks of 9/11. As a response to the attacks, the United States passed the Homeland Security Act and launched wars in Afghanistan and Iraq to protect against future terrorist attacks. A consequence of increased institutional vigilance against terrorism were public perceptions, reinforced by imagery in popular culture and the media, that Muslims were terrorists and that increased public and private vigilance against them was not only justified but to be encouraged (Alimahomed-Wilson, 2017). Muslim women, in particular, are particularly vulnerable to increased surveillance, discriminatory treatment, and victimization because they are visible symbols of Islam.

Contributing to the victimization of Muslim women was an ideology in the United States and most of the West that defined the societal role of a woman as independent, free, and resistant to male dominance. In contrast, the image of Muslim women cultivated in Western popular culture including news and entertainment and accepted by large majorities in Western countries (Perry, 2014; Allen, 2015) was one of powerlessness, vulnerability, oppression, willing or coerced accomplices of terrorists, and mysterious, sexualized objects of male domination (Perry, 2014). These images and the resulting stereotypes (chapters 2 and 3 of this book) have led to an ideology popular in many Western countries that Muslim women need to be saved from Muslim men (Perry, 2014).

Ironically, Muslim women are considered to be helpless and in need of saving, but at the same time are objects of hate because they are "different," "don't belong," and are a threat (Perry, 2014). Although acts of aggression toward Muslim women have increased significantly in the last decade (Pew, 2017), most people do not admit that they are biased toward Muslims. A recent national random sample, for example, showed that 70% of American adults agree with Muslim Americans (75%) that there is "a lot" of discrimination against Muslims in the US (Pew Research Center, 2017). It's not likely that Americans sympathizing with Muslim Americans will hold explicit negative perceptions of Muslims and Muslim women. Nevertheless, as decades of research on implicit biases show (Nosek et al., 2011), possibly up to 80% of Americans have implicit racial biases which, when activated, can direct evaluations and actions toward the targeted groups. Most Americans may not have explicit biases toward Muslim women, but a large majority most likely have implicit biases which can be activated by environmental primes such as head and face coverings.

RESPONSES OF MUSLIM WOMEN TO HATE

Most Muslim women who are victims of hate aggression do not report the experiences to the police (Allen, 2015). In Europe, 59% of Muslim women experiencing hateful aggression chose not to report (Allen, 2015). The major reason is distrust of the police, as revealed in in-depth interviews and focus groups (Allen, 2015), and the perception that the police would not recognize the severity of the aggressions and therefore would not understand their concerns (Zempi, 2016). In addition, many Muslim women did not feel comfortable being interrogated by the police, particularly by men, and that women interviewers would not be available. Lack of confidence in the police stems from doubts among the women that the police would have knowledge—any knowledge—of Islam (Zempi, 2016).

Instead of reporting anti-Muslim aggressions to the police, Muslim women are more likely to report their experiences to community-based third-party organizations (Allen, 2015). The British government, for example, funded the creation of a community organization called Measuring Anti-Muslim Attacks (MAMA). Victims can report the hate incidents in person or electronically by email, SMS, Twitter, Facebook, and a MAMA website. MAMA sends the information to police authorities for possible processing. Through this process, Muslim women are provided a friendly organization they trust to whom they can report their experiences (Allen, 2015).

In many studies in Europe and the United States, the most common response of Muslim women to hateful aggression is to ignore the experiences and move on with their lives (Zempi, 2016). Reasons for ignoring the aggressions are the women got used to them, that they would not like to dignify the actions by a response and responding aggressively would be contrary to Islam (Zempi, 2016). These reasons are not to be interpreted as passive compliance but rather as a choice to be true to the principles of Islam. The few women who respond aggressively do so verbally (to the aggressor—"Well, if I had a face like yours I would never want to take my veil off"; "Yeah, I am a terrorist, do you want to see my gun?; "What the f. . . are you looking at") or physically (giving the finger; pushing back). Muslim women who respond by confronting their aggressors say it's because they had had enough, that it was their personality, and they wanted to make a point that Muslim women were not passive (Zempi, 2016).

The variety of responses to hateful aggression demonstrates that public perceptions of Muslim women as a homogenous group conforming to popular stereotypes are inaccurate. Rather than being passive and without agency, Muslim women demonstrate in their actions that they are doing so in conscious choice.

Regardless of their immediate response, many Muslim women say they have changed some behaviors to feel safer in public spaces. These changes include not venturing out of their homes as frequently; going in the company of other Muslim women; going to places they consider to be "safe" such as shopping malls and neighborhoods with Muslims and racial minorities. Some Muslim women have reported not wearing the hijab or other Islamic fashion when venturing into public places (Zempi, 2016; Allen, 2015; Perry, 2014.)

Another consequence to Muslim women of aggressive harassment are emotions, the most common being anger and fear. These emotions are short-term and do not necessarily lead to long-term depression and anxiety (Allen, 2015). Other emotions are annoyance, shock, vulnerability, and anxiety. Fear from aggressive encounters lead to generalized fear of profiling and of appearing in public which in turn lead to coping mechanisms such as less frequent appearances in public, selecting public places where they feel safe, unwillingness to appear in public alone, and not wearing the hijab, the niqab or burka. The women, by engaging in these coping strategies, are prioritizing their safety over their expression of identity and independence (Perry, 2014).

PREJUDICE IN EMPLOYMENT

Studies of employment discrimination against Muslims in seven Western European countries, Canada, Australia, and the United States consistently show that Muslim job applicants are less likely to be evaluated positively or hired compared to non-Muslim, mainstream, generally White, job applicants (Bartkoski et al., 2018). Discrimination is demonstrated in negative behaviors by hiring officials toward Muslim applicants such as callbacks, formal responses to a job application, length of interaction, greetings, recommendation for the position, or being told the job is no longer available. Discrimination is also demonstrated by interpersonal evaluations such as liking or disliking, perceived "fit"; perceived general competence and qualifications; and perceived suitability for the job (Ghumman & Ryan, 2013).

Although employment discrimination does not differ significantly for Muslim women and non-Muslim women, Muslim women in hijabs, niqabs, or burqas have a much lower likelihood of employment than Muslim women who do not wear hijab (religious clothing in general). Muslim women in hijab are 40% to 20% less likely to be hired (Abdelhadi, 2019). As with non-Muslim women, barriers to employment include demographics (age and ethnicity), education, and household composition (marriage and childbearing). For Muslim women in hijab, stereotypes and negative perceptions are major contributors to employment discrimination.

Muslim women's religious attire are identifiable signifiers of Islam. To most Westerners, the hijab, niqab, and burqa activate negative gendered perceptions and stereotypes of Muslim women. A series of experiments comparing implicit and explicit biases elicited by a Muslim woman with no veil, with a hijab, and with a niqab showed that in comparison to the woman with no veil, the women with a hijab and niqab elicited more negative emotions (anger, irritation, and annoyance), less positive emotions (admiration, trust, warm); less empathy ("seeing the world through this person's eyes," " could understand what it's like to be this person"; more negative expectations of interaction ("she would interpret my behavior as prejudiced"); greater implicit biases as measured by the IAT (weaker associations with positive words such as cheer, freedom, friend, happy, health, honest, love, loyal, peace, pleasure, and stronger associations with negative words such as bomb, crash, death, disaster, evil, grief, hatred, kill, prison, tragedy) (Everett et al., 2015). The studies showed more negative perceptions of the woman wearing a niqab compared to the woman in a hijab for emotions and implicit biases. These results provide evidence that Muslim women in religious head and face coverings activate biases that can affect employment evaluations and behaviors.

In the next chapter, we discuss three original studies about primes of Muslim women and employment discrimination.

Chapter 6

Semantic and Visual Primes of Stereotypes of Muslim Women

Activation and Activation Control

In this chapter, we discuss three studies investigating the effects of hijab as media primes on the activation of stereotypes of Muslim women and on the activation of stereotype use in evaluations for employment. The first two studies were presented at national conferences of the Association for Education in Journalism and Mass Communication (Tan, Vishnevskaya, & Khan, 2019; Vishnevskaya, Khan, & Tan, 2020). The third study, an extension of Study 2, is presented for the first time in this book.

SEMANTIC AND VISUAL PRIMES OF MUSLIM WOMEN: EVALUATIVE AND BEHAVIORAL CONSEQUENCES

"Think about it: Omar wears a hijab. Is her adherence to this Islamic doctrine indicative of her adherence to Sharia law which in itself is antithetical to the United States Constitution?" former Fox News host Jeanine Pirro, March 2019, referring to U.S. Representative Ilhan Omar, D-MN. (as quoted by Pintak, Bowe, & Albright, 2019)

The effects of media and other environmental primes like Representative Omar's hijab on stereotyping of out-groups such as racial and ethnic minorities are consistent and well documented in the research literature. In its simplest formulation, primes are stimuli that either elicit or add to cognitive structures of groups in perceivers. Also referred to as schemas and stereotypes, these structures define groups by assigning character, personality, and behavioral traits to all group members with few or no exceptions (e.g.,

Blair & Banaji, 1996; Muller & Rothermund, 2014; Arendt, 2013; Kidder, White, Hinojos, Sandoval, & Crites Jr., 2018). Some common findings are that primes—which can be semantic (e.g., a name associated with a racial group) or visual (e.g., a photograph of a racial group member)—reinforce stereotypes stored in long-term memory, elicit evaluative responses, and direct behaviors consistent with stored stereotypes. Most communication researchers investigate stereotype reinforcement by primes (e.g., Arendt, 2013) while most social psychologists investigate the evaluative and behavioral consequences of primes as automatic responses (e.g., Eberhardt, Goff, Purdue & Davies, 2004).

More recently, attention in communication and social psychology has focused on moderating variables that might refine monotonic predictions regarding the influence of primes.

One variable generating interest in communication is "prime intensity," defined as dose (Arendt, 2013), frequency (Iyengar, Kinder, Peters & Krosnick, 1984), or strength (Carpenter, Roskos-Ewoldson, & Roskos-Ewoldson, 2008). Social psychologists are interested in the unconscious emotional and cognitive processes that explain automatic responses to a single prime or a series of primes (e.g., Muller & Rothermund, 2014).

In communication and psychology, researchers have recently turned their attention to negation of strong primes and how negation can lead to rejection of stereotypes and less negative evaluations of the stereotyped group. Arendt (2013), for example found that heavy and repeated associations of immigrant groups with crime in newspaper stories led to a rejection of the "immigrant as criminal" stereotype among her college student respondents. Rachilinski et al. (2009) found that their panel of judges showed no bias in adjudicating hypothetical criminal cases involving Black and White defendants. They explained their results as successful attempts by judges to negate common stereotypes associating Blacks with crime. In their study, photos of Black and White suspects were used as primes. Interest in negation of stereotypes triggered by strong primes has led to the development of prejudice-reduction strategies to reduce harmful consequences of bias (e.g., Tan, 2021).

In Study 1, we combine theoretical approaches from communication and social psychology. From the communication perspective, we investigate prime intensity as a moderator of prime responses. Drawing from theories of the cognitive processing of signs and symbols (e.g., Lang, 2000), we study the relative influence of verbal and visual primes on reinforcing stereotypes.

Taking a social psychological approach, we investigate the influence of primes on the automatic activation of related responses other than stereotypes (e.g., Blair & Banaji, 1996; Kidder et al., 2018.) We test the influence of primes on evaluations and behavioral intentions.

Using activation control theory (e.g., Arendt, 2013; Nosek, Greenwald & Banaji, 2007), we ask whether a single dose of a strong prime can result in negation of the stereotype and related evaluations of the "target" group.

Our "target" group is Muslim women, a minority group not well understood and often the object of negative stereotyping, discrimination, and hate crimes in the West (e.g., Janson, 2011; Terman, 2017). We ask two research questions:

RQ 1: Will semantic and visual primes have differential effects on stereotypes, evaluations of, and intention to hire a Muslim woman applicant for a university teaching position? RQ1 leads to a hypothesis that the relationship between primes, stereotypes, and evaluations will be linear: the more intense the prime, the more negative the stereotypes and evaluations of the target group. We present theories and results from previous studies that semantic primes are low intensity while visual primes are high intensity.

RQ 2: Will a strong single visual prime lead to negation effects, that is, rejection of negative stereotypes and related evaluations of the target group? RQ2 leads to a hypothesis that the relationship between prime intensity, stereotypes, and evaluations of the target group is curvilinear: that is, the most negative stereotypes and evaluations will be observed in the moderate prime condition, with moderately negative stereotypes and evaluations in the low and high prime conditions.

We test these competing hypotheses in a one-factor laboratory experiment conducted online with college student participants. Although not common, we test competing hypothesis in one study because both are firmly based on theory and have not been previously tested in the same study.

PRIMING THEORIES AND RESEARCH[1]

Priming theories conceptualize primes as stimuli in the environment that are connected to schematic information (e.g., stereotypes) stored in long-term memory. The perceiver makes this connection consciously, as when explicit stereotypes are activated, or unconsciously, as when implicit stereotypes are activated (Blair & Banaji, 1996). In most communication research (see Abraham & Appiah, 2006, for an exception), primes are operationalized as semantic codes in mediated narratives (e.g., a news story) that connect events, explicitly or implicitly, to a stereotype target (e.g., Arendt, 2013). Most priming research in social psychology operationalize primes as a single semantic code (e.g., a name or word associated with the target group) or a single visual code (e.g., a photograph of a target group) in one exposure or a series of exposures. The operating theoretical principle in communication and social psychology is that stereotypes are stored in long-term memory and can either be reinforced or activated by primes currently encountered.

MEDIA PRIMES

Numerous studies including a meta-analysis of media priming research (Roskos-Ewoldson, Klinger, & Roskos-Ewoldson, 2007) have established that media primes, defined as biased representations of out-groups such as racial minorities, produce and reinforce stereotypes of those groups (e.g., Ramasubramanian, 2007). These effects can be explained by theories of media cultivation (Signorielli, Morgan, & Shanahan, 2019) and social learning (Bandura, 2002). Consciously or unconsciously, the perceiver incorporates new information from media primes into existing cognitive structures about the stereotype target. More recently, research in communication has differentiated between priming effects on explicit and implicit stereotypes allowing for the possibility that frequent exposure might not be an adequate explanation of effects. With the development of measures such as the Implicit Association Test (IAT) (e.g., Greenwald, Poehlman, Uhlmann & Banaji, 2009), recent research has differentiated between priming effects on explicit and implicit stereotypes. Cultivation theories, in particular, predict a monotonic effect: that is, frequent exposure leads to stronger stereotypes.

Theories of activation control, on the other hand, predict that perceivers can reject or negate new information supporting negative stereotypes stored in memory because of social pressure, self-concept reinforcement, norms, and other forms of social control (e.g., Blair & Banaji, 1996). Therefore, activation control theories predict that perceivers will reject the new negative information in the stereotype primes after a threshold is reached. Arendt (2013) operationalizes this threshold as "dose."

Providing evidence for a threshold effect, she found a monotonic effect of dose on implicit stereotypes; that is, the more exposure to news stories linking an out-group to a negative event, the stronger the implicit stereotypes. On the other hand, she found a curvilinear effect for explicit stereotypes: stereotyping increased up to a threshold (moderate exposure to negative news stories), after which stereotyping decreased. She explained these findings in terms of activation control theory. Heavy doses of priming made perceivers aware of their own explicit stereotypes and led them to control their biases. For explicit stereotypes, priming led to increased stereotyping up to a moderate threshold, then decreased with heavy priming. Explicit stereotypes are openly and publicly acknowledged; motivation to control them can be triggered by strong primes. In contrast, people are unaware of implicit stereotypes and biases and are not motivated to control these biases unless they are made aware of them (Blair & Banaji, 1996).

DISCRETE SEMANTIC AND VISUAL PRIMES

The power of discrete semantic primes (such as a name or word associated with a target group) and discrete visual primes (such as a photograph of a target group member) to activate implicit stereotypes and related evaluations and behaviors is well established (see, for example, Schneider, 2004; Kidder et al., 2018). The underlying theoretical principles are that most people (80%, according to Nosek, Greenwald & Banaji, 2007) have stored implicit stereotypes in long-term memory; that these implicit biases can be activated by the mere presence of stimuli in the environment; that the activation is automatic, unconscious, not under the control of the perceiver and therefore not the result of conscious information processing. Activation is demonstrated in the automatic and unconscious association of stereotypical traits with cues related to the target group (such as a name or photo), or the association of target group cues with stereotypical evaluations and behavioral intentions (Blair & Banaji, 1996; Eberhardt et al., 2004).

NAMES AS PRIMES

A number of studies support the prediction that a discrete semantic prime such as a name can activate evaluations of a job candidate. The assumption is that the race of an applicant can be surmised from the applicant's name, leading to the automatic and unconscious activation of stereotypes associated with the racial group. In a field experiment involving 5,000 resumes and 1,300 employment ads in Chicago and Boston newspapers, Bertrand & Mullainathan (2004) found that applicants with White names needed to send 10 resumes to get one callback, whereas applicants with African American names sending identical resumes as White applicants needed to send 15 resumes. Also, Whites with higher quality resumes received nearly 30% more callbacks compared to Whites with lower quality resumes, while the difference among Blacks was not significant.

Similar results were found for Arab-Muslim names by Rooth (2010) in a study in Sweden. Applicants with Swedish names were more likely to be invited for an interview than applicants with Arab-Muslim names, holding constant the quality of resumes. Furthermore, Rooth (2010) found that job recruiters who had at least moderate negative implicit biases toward Muslims as measured by the IAT were the most likely to demonstrate hiring bias.

The influence of name primes extends to gender hiring biases. Moss-Racusin, Dovidio, Brescoll, Graham & Handelsman (2012) asked 127 professors in the sciences to rate the application of an undergraduate student applying for a science laboratory position. The resumes were identical. In half of the resumes, the applicant was assigned a female name and in the other half, the name of a male. Moss-Racusin et al. (2012) found that both men and women evaluators rated the male applicant as more competent and hirable than the female applicant, recommended a higher salary for the male applicant, and offered more career mentoring to the male applicant.

Taken together, these studies present compelling evidence that a single discrete verbal prime—a name identifying target group membership—influences evaluations of and behavioral intention toward a group member. According to stereotype activation theory, the name primes unconscious biases and stereotypes which in turn direct evaluations and intended actions. This explanation is supported, for example, by Rooth (2010) finding that implicit stereotypes magnified the hiring biases of job recruiters.

PHOTOGRAPHS AS PRIMES

According to stereotype activation theories, the mere presence of a target group member can prompt a perceiver to associate unconscious stereotypes with the target group. The activation of latent stereotypes influences responses without the perceiver's awareness (Blair & Banaji, 1996). In most studies, photographs substitute for actual presence. A number of studies provide evidence that photographs activate implicit stereotypes, stereotypic evaluations, and behavioral intentions.

For example, analysis of skin color and implicit stereotypes using the IAT consistently shows that dark skin, Blacks in particular, in photographs is associated with danger, violence, and crime (Greenwald & Krieger, 2006). The IAT measures response time in milliseconds—the less time, the stronger the automatic association between photographs and stereotypical words and objects. A consistent finding is that Black faces in photographs in comparison to White faces, is more strongly (takes less time) associated with violent objects, crime, and danger. Similarly, Arab-Muslim faces are more strongly associated with violence and terrorism.

Using photographs as primes, IATs also show that most people associate women more strongly with liberal arts and men with science; women with family, and men with careers; Asian Americans with foreign landmarks and European Americans with American landmarks (Nosek, Greenwald & Banaji, 2007). In these IATs, photographs of target groups are used as primes; implicit stereotypes are represented by photographs or words. Automatic prime and stereotype associations are explained as activation of implicit stereotypes which the perceiver does not have conscious control over. The influence of photographic primes extends from activation of implicit stereotypes to the activation of group evaluations and related behaviors.

Eberhardt, Goff, Purdie & Davies (2004) found that Black male faces facilitated the identification of crime-related objects as well as abstract concepts stereotypically associated with Black men (crime and basketball.) Study participants were police officers and college undergraduates.

In Germany, Gawronski, Gerschke & Banse (2003) found that photos of Turkish-looking young men attached to a brief description of ambiguous behaviors (e,g, young men partying) elicited more negative evaluations of the behaviors compared to identical behaviors with photos of German-looking young men.

Oliver and Fonash (2002) showed college student participants photos of Black and White suspects in news stories, as well as photos of Black and White young men who were not suspects. They found that Blacks, more often than Whites, were misidentified as suspects in the violent crime news stories.

Correll, Park, Judd & Wittenbrink (2007) instructed their college student participants to "shoot" an armed target and "don't shoot" an unarmed target in a video game by pressing the appropriate computer key. Half of the targets were Black; half were White. They found that (a) participants "shot" Black targets, unarmed and armed, more frequently than White targets; (b) participants more quickly "shot" an armed target when he was Black than when he was White; (c) participants more quickly did not "shoot" an unarmed target when he was White than when he was Black.

Photograph primes activate not only evaluations and behaviors but also opinions on public policy issues. Abraham and Appiah (2006) found that online news stories about three strikes crime laws and school vouchers were more strongly associated with Blacks when accompanied by photos of Blacks compared to when accompanied by photos of Whites. As explained by the authors, the photos primed implicit stereotypes which were then projected unto the policy issues.

CULTURE AS SOURCE OF STEREOTYPES

While media priming studies look at media news and entertainment as sources of explicit and implicit stereotypes (e.g., Arendt, 2013), studies of the activation of implicit stereotypes look at "culture" more broadly as a source of implicit stereotypes (Verhaeghen, Aikman & Van Gulick, 2011). The priming of implicit stereotypes is dependent on the existence in long-term memory of stereotypes to be primed. Culture is often identified as a common source. Jones (1997), for example, gives a definition of cultural racism that is applicable to implicit stereotypes:

> Cultural racism is . . . the cumulative effect of a racialized worldview, based on belief in essential racial differences that favor the dominant racial group over others. These effects are suffused throughout the culture via institutional structures, ideological beliefs, and personal everyday actions of people in the culture, and these effects are passed on from generation to generation. (p. 472)

Cultural influence on stereotypes is often conceptualized as the sum total of influences from socialization agents including parents, school, peers, the media, the community, personal experiences, and social and political institutions (e.g., government) (Verhaeghen et al., 2011; Rudman, 2004; Devine, 1989). Although socialization is a life-long process, most adults have stored in long-term memory implicit stereotypes of groups which can be activated by primes.

INTENSITY: SEMANTIC AND VISUAL PRIMES

Theories of the automatic activation of stereotypes generally require only one prime. On the other hand, theories of media priming suggest that prime intensity moderates the relationship between primes in the media and stereotypes. The intensity of primes depends on frequency, dose, and length (Arendt, 2013). Prime modality—whether the prime is semantic or visual—can also influence the strength of the association between primes and the activation of stereotypes. Research comparing the relative influence on memory and emotions of words and pictures show that visual imagery is more powerful in activating stereotypes than words alone (Abraham, 1998, 2003.) Visual images evoke involuntary, unconscious, and uncontrolled responses in receivers (Blair, Judd, & Chapleau, 2004). Some research suggests that humans are hardwired to respond to visual stimuli. To preserve the species, humans relied on vision to survive and adapt to the environment as, for example, in choosing a mate and identifying predators and food sources (Medina, 2008). Studies supporting this view show that "pictures have a direct route to long-term memory, each image storing its own information as a coherent chunk or concept" (Medina, 2008, p. 2.) Although primes operate at an unconscious or subliminal level of attention (e.g., Eberhardt et al.,

2004), the implication is that visuals such as photographs will be more likely transported to existing cognitive structures than words because they are more easily accessed and attended to. Therefore, photos and other visuals will be more powerful primes than words (e.g., Abraham & Appiah, 2006; Eberhardt et al., 2004).

STEREOTYPES OF MUSLIM WOMEN

The prevalent stereotypes of Muslims in post 9/11 America link Muslims and Islam to terrorism, violence, extremism, and characterize them as culturally distinct, a threat to Western values (Kalkan, Layman, & Uslaner, 2009; Pew Research Center, 2014). In a more nuanced analysis, Sides and Gross (2013) found a binary configuration of Muslim stereotypes. Drawing on the 2004 American National Election Study (ANES), they found that Muslims scored third lowest—closest to "very cold"—in a Feeling Thermometer Scale. Only gays and lesbians and illegal immigrants scored lower. Data from the 2006 and 2007 Cooperative Congressional Election Studies (CCES) indicate that random nationwide samples of American adults attributed the traits "hardworking," "intelligent," "violent," and "untrustworthy" to Muslims, a mixture of positive and negative stereotypes. Sides and Gross (2013) concluded that Muslim stereotypes consist of two dimensions: competence (hardworking and intelligent) and warmth (peaceful and trustworthy). American adults perceive Muslims to be competent but not warm. These stereotypes, particularly the warmth dimension, direct evaluations and opinions. For example, respondents who rated Muslims low on the warmth dimension were the most likely to support public policies supporting the War on Terror such as decreased spending on foreign aid, increased spending on border security, and increased spending on the War on Terror (Sides & Gross, 2013).

Like most stereotypes in general, Western perceptions of Muslim women as oppressed, misogynistic, and without personal agency are not necessarily grounded in reality. For the most part, these perceptions are based on biased portrayals in the media including frequent use of visual symbols (such as clothing) that accentuate differences and reinforce out-group distinctions. Lost in media narratives is the wide variety in values, beliefs, behaviors, and personal accomplishments of Muslim women who are not unlike all other women in their diversity. Soltani (2016) provides an example of this diversity in her analysis of why Muslim women wear a hijab:

During the European colonial period, for example, the hijab was worn by Muslim women as a sign of anti-colonial resistance to reaffirm their identity and culture. Several studies in the UK and the US also reveal that for some Muslim women, Islamic dress and the veil function as strong statements of identity. For Muslim women living in Europe and the United States, wearing the veil is a way of forming an ethno-religious identity—a way of belonging." (p. 5)

In summary, Muslim women's clothing are symbols in the West of an out-group, a threat to native cultures. Hijabs, veils, and burqas, because they provide unusual and unique visual images, can prime implicit stereotypes, evaluations, and behaviors toward Muslim women.

STUDY 1

In the present study, we test the differential effects of Muslim women primes on explicit stereotypes, evaluations, and behavioral intent. A fundamental principle from stereotype activation theory guides our study: stereotypes and related evaluative and behavioral responses can be activated by single exposure, discrete semantic, and visual primes. Following recent findings from media priming research, we test whether prime intensity affects response strength. Rather than using the IAT, we measured stereotypes, evaluations, and behavioral intent with a questionnaire. Therefore, our measures tapped explicit responses, leading to the possibility of curvilinear predictions of the influence of prime intensity (Arendt, 2013).

We used a laboratory experiment conducted online with four levels of one factor. The factor is prime intensity. Based on theory and research on semantic and visual primes, and our discussion on Muslim women and clothing, the low-intensity prime is a typical Muslim woman's name; the moderate intensity prime is the Muslim name accompanied by a photograph of a Muslim women; the high-intensity prime is the Muslim name accompanied by a photograph of the same Muslim woman wearing a hijab. We added a control condition using a name prime that is typically European American. Following previous studies on names and employment bias (e.g., Bertrand & Mullainathan, 2004; Rooth, 2010; Moss-Racusin et al., 2012) we presented the primes to our college student participants in a job application for a university faculty position.

The application consisted of a curriculum vitae (CV). Dependent variables were stereotypes of Muslim women, evaluation of the applicant for the job, and behavioral intentions to hire.

Following cultivation and social learning theories (RQ 1), we tested for a linear relationship between prime intensity and the dependent variables. Specifically, we tested the following hypotheses:

H1: Compared to the control prime (European American name), the low-intensity prime (Muslim name) will be stereotyped more negatively, evaluated more negatively for the job, and will be less likely to be interviewed and hired.

H2: Compared to the low-intensity prime (Muslim name), the moderate prime (photo of a Muslim woman) will be stereotyped more negatively, evaluated more negatively for the job, and will be less likely to be interviewed and hired.

H3: Compared to the moderate prime (photo of a Muslim woman), the high-intensity prime (photo of same Muslim woman wearing a hijab) will be stereotyped more negatively, evaluated less positively for the job, and will be less likely to be interviewed and hired.

Following Activation Control Theory (RQ 2), we tested another set of competing hypotheses:

H4: Compared to the low-intensity prime, the moderate intensity prime will be stereotyped and evaluated more negatively and will be less likely to be interviewed and hired.

H5: Compared to the moderate intensity prime, the high-intensity prime will be stereotyped and evaluated less negatively and will be more likely to be interviewed and hired.

Method

Participants

Undergraduate students in communication at a large public university participated in the study ($N = 109$). We recruited the participants from a College of Communication research participant pool using the SONA system. SONA identifies students who have volunteered to participate in research projects by college faculty and graduate students. The students receive extra credit in classes for participation.

Design

We used a randomized between-subjects' laboratory experiment with four levels (control, low-intensity prime, moderate intensity prime, high-intensity prime) of one factor (prime intensity). We randomly assigned participants to one of the four conditions, resulting in 26–28 participants per group. For these group sizes, we estimate power ($1 - B$) to be about 0.5 and effect size to be less than 0.5 (medium) (Muller & Rothermund, 2014). We presented the study to participants as an evaluation of a candidate for a faculty position at the university (location of the study). We instructed them to read the position announcement and the applicant's CV before completing a questionnaire. Each group received only one condition—a CV with a European American name; a CV with a Muslim name; a CV with the Muslim name and a photo of the applicant without a hijab; and a CV with a Muslim name and a photo of the applicant with a hijab. Participants completed the study online at their own time. We used Qualtrics to record questionnaire responses. The dependent variables were stereotypes of Muslim women, evaluations of the applicant for the faculty position, and intention to hire the applicant.

Stimulus Materials

The stimuli (factor levels) represented low, moderate, and high prime intensities plus a control condition without a Muslim prime. The low-intensity prime was a Muslim woman's name (Azhaar Basheera) accompanying the CV. The moderate prime was a photo accompanying the CV with the Muslim name. The high-intensity prime was a photo of the same woman wearing a hijab (a veil covering her head, hair, ears, and neck), accompanying the CV. The control condition was a CV with a European American name (Elizabeth Fitzgerald). The CVs were identical in all conditions and included qualifications addressing position requirements in the announcement (see Appendix A for the position announcement and the CV of the applicant).

We chose the Muslim name from a directory of typical names for Muslim women (e.g., Sides & Gross, 2013); the European American name was from a directory of typical names for Irish American women. We selected the photo of the Muslim woman from a previous study validating her facial features as typically Middle Eastern. The hijab was added by Photoshop.

Validation of our operationalization of prime intensity is provided by theories and studies reviewed earlier in this chapter. Visual primes such as photographs elicit stronger emotional and cognitive responses than semantic primes such as names. The hijab presents a strong visible sign of a "foreign" culture that contrasts with Western cultures.

Dependent Measures

We measured stereotypes of Muslim women, evaluations for the job, and behavioral intentions to hire as our dependent variables. For stereotypes, we used a 7-point semantic differential with nine bipolar adjectives representing "warmth" and "competence" dimensions adapted from Sides and Gross (2013). The warmth adjectives were warm/cold, friendly/not friendly, can be trusted/cannot be trusted, likable/not likable, and pleasant/not pleasant. The competence adjectives were competent/not competent, hardworking/not hardworking, knowledgeable/not knowledgeable, articulate/not articulate. We added an overall evaluation: would be a good colleague/would not be a good colleague. To avoid response bias, we alternated positive and negative traits in the scales. We scored the ratings for each item from 1 (most negative) to 7 (most positive) and summed the item scores for all adjectives and separately for the warmth and competence dimensions.

We measured evaluations of the applicant for the job and intention to hire with questions adapted from Bertrand and Mullainathan (2004), Rooth (2010) and Moss-Racusin et al. (2012).

These items were:

Competence:
"How qualified is this candidate for the position? not qualified at all, not qualified, don't know, qualified, very qualified."

Warmth:
"How well do you think this candidate would interact with students? very well, quite well, don't know, not too well, not well at all."
"How well do you think this candidate would interact with other faculty? very well, quite well, don't know, not too well, not well at all."

Behavioral Intent:
"Would you invite this candidate to campus for an interview? definitely no, most likely no, don't know, most likely yes, definitely yes."
"Would you hire this candidate for the position? Definitely no, most likely no, don't know, most likely yes, definitely yes."

We summed the scores separately for the evaluation items measuring warmth and competence, and for the behavioral items measuring intent to interview and intent to hire, from 1 (most negative response) to 5 (most positive response).

In summary, we measured and computed the following sets of dependent variables:

1. Stereotypes, warmth adjectives
2. Stereotypes, competence adjectives
3. Stereotype: overall trait (would be a good colleague)
4. Evaluation for the job: competence item
5. Evaluation for the job: warmth items
6. Behavioral intent: intent to interview; intent to hire

Procedure

The study was conducted online. Participants read the experimental protocols and answered the questionnaire individually and on their own time. To ensure that instructions were followed, we imposed time restrictions on completion of certain tasks (see below).

We identified college student participants through a SONA system administered by the authors' home college, sent them a link to the study which included instructions, the experimental and control conditions, and a questionnaire measuring the dependent variables. The questionnaire used Qualtrics; responses were recorded into an SPSS file for analysis. We told the participants that the purpose of the study is "to evaluate an applicant for an instructor position in the College of Communication."

Participants were randomly assigned to one of four conditions: low-intensity prime (CV with Muslim name), moderate intensity prime (CV, Muslim name, and photo), high-intensity prime (CV, Muslim name, and photo with hijab), and a control group (CV with a European American name). The participants received identical CVs. To ensure that our participants read the position announcement and CVs before answering the questionnaire, we required at least 10 seconds before they could click on to proceed.

Analysis

We used MANOVA to detect main effects of prime intensity on each of the dependent variables. Additionally, we used paired-samples t tests to detect differences between groups.

Results

Participants

The original pool consisted of 118 college students who volunteered for the study. Nine were excluded in the analysis because they indicated familiarity with the study. After completing the protocols and questionnaire, they said, in answer to a question, that the purpose of the study was "priming" and/ or "stereotypes." The study pool was 109 participants: 81 White students (74.31%), 28 (25.68%) non-Whites; 27 males and 82 females. After listwise deletion of missing responses, there were a total of 106 valid cases.

Independent Variable

We assigned the 106 valid cases randomly to four groups representing the priming intensity factor plus a control. Distribution was fairly equal: Group 1 (control, Irish American Name) = 28; Group 2 (low prime, Middle Eastern name) = 26; Group 3 (moderate prime, Middle Eastern name plus photo) = 26; Group 4 (high prime, Middle Eastern name plus photo with hijab).

Dependent Variables

We tested for the effects of priming intensity on five dependent variables: Perception of Qualification (M = 4.17, SD = 0.66, one item measured on a 5-point scale, 5 = "very qualified"); Intention to Hire (M = 3.94, SD = 0.637, 2 items measured on a 5-point scale, 5 = "definitely yes," Cronbach's alpha = 0.76); Job Warmth (M = 3.89, SD = 0.69, 2 items measured on a 5-point scale, 5 = most warm); Cronbach's alpha = 0.84; Stereotype Warmth (M = 5.55, SD = 1.01, 5 semantic differential scales, 7 = most warm, Cronbach's alpha = 0.927); Stereotype Competence (M = 18.83, SD = 3.37; 4 semantic differential scales, 7 = most competent, Cronbach's alpha = 0.913.) The Skewness and Kurtosis statistics for each of the five variables are within the range of +2 and −2, indicative of normality. Levine's test indicates that the assumption of univariate homogeneity has been met too.

Tests of Competing Hypotheses

We used MANOVA to test two sets of hypotheses. Hypotheses 1 to 3 predicted that evaluations and stereotypes of Muslim women would diminish in a linear fashion from control to high prime conditions. Hypotheses 4 and 5, on the other hand predict evaluations and stereotypes would be lowest in the moderate prime group. We test these hypotheses for each of the five dependent variables.

Job Warmth: Analysis of main effects showed that priming intensity had a significant influence on job warmth evaluation (F, 1, 102 = 4.33, p = 0.006). Table 6.1 shows that group means support a curvilinear relationship between prime intensity job warmth which was highest in the high prime condition, and lowest in low prime. The difference in means between low prime and high prime is significant at $p < 0.05$ (Scheffé test). Although significant main effects indicate that the factor explains a significant proportion of the dependent variable, a posteriori tests of paired means may not show significance

Table 6.1   Means of Job Applicant Evaluations by Priming Dose

	Control (Group1)	Low Prime (Group2)	Medium Prime (Group3)	High Prime (Group4)
Perception of Qualification	4.03	4.00	4.23	4.46
Intention to Hire	3.90	3.82	3.98	4.077
Job Warmth Evaluation	3.79	3.59*	4.02	4.19*
Stereotype Warmth	5.1**	5.58	5.78	5.84**
Stereotype Competence	18.24	18.57	18.99	19.62

*Group means differ on both Tukey HSD and Scheffé test at $p < 0.05$.
**Group means differ using only Tukey HSD test at $p < 0.05$.

because of low power (more than 0.5), a result of relatively group sizes less than 30 (e.g., Muller & Rothermund, 2014).

Stereotype Warmth: We also found significant main effects of priming intensity on stereotype warmth evaluation (F, 1, 102 = 2.946, p = 0.036.) Table 6.1 shows that the group means support a linear relationship between prime intensity and stereotype warmth, but in the opposite direction predicted by our first set of hypotheses (least warm = high prime.) The evaluation was most warm in the high-intensity prime. The relationship is not curvilinear, since evaluations linearly increase from the control, low prime, moderate prime, and high prime groups. The difference between the control and high prime groups is significant at $p<0.05$ (Scheffé test).

Qualifications

The main effect for the influence of prime intensity on perceived qualifications is significant (F, 1, 102 = 2.706, p = 0.049). Table 6.1 shows that the group means follow a similar pattern as for Job:

Warmth: High Prime had the highest ratings for Qualifications, and low prime, the lowest, indicative of a curvilinear relationship.

Intent to Hire: The main effect for Intent to Hire is not significant. Although not significant, the pattern of group means is similar to Job Warmth and Qualifications. The highest ratings were by the High Prime Group; the lowest ratings were by the Low Prime Group.

Stereotype Competence: Although the main effect was not significant, group means showed a similar pattern as for Stereotype Warmth. Evaluations progressively increased to more positive as priming intensity increased.

Discussion, Conclusions, Limitations

Our study provides support for hypotheses derived from Activation Control Theory. A single dose of a heavy photographic prime (photograph of a Muslim woman wearing a hijab) resulted in the most positive stereotypes and evaluations of a job applicant, particularly for the warmth dimensions. The relationship between prime dose stereotypes and evaluations appears to be curvilinear in most cases: there was a dip for the moderate prime condition from the control and low prime conditions, then an increase in the high prime condition. In some cases, the relationship was linear but in the opposite direction predicted by cultivation and social learning theories: ratings accelerated linearly, from negative to positive, with the most positive ratings in the high prime condition. We observed these patterns for all dependent variables, even when main effects were not significant.

On the other hand, we found no support for hypotheses based on cultivation and social learning theories. Stereotypes and evaluations did not decrease (become more negative) with prime intensity. We therefore conclude that within the parameters of the present study, a high-intensity prime triggered activation control of negative stereotypes and evaluation biases, leading to more positive stereotypes and evaluations of a Muslim woman. We offer several explanations for these findings and conclusions:

1. Compared to the general population, college students are more open-minded and more motivated to control biases (e.g., Nosek, Greenwald & Banaji, 2007). Therefore, they are more likely to negate biases associated with high-intensity primes.
2. Compared to men, women are less likely to be biased and more motivated to control their biases (e.g., Nosek, Greenwald & Banaji, 2007). Our participant pool was over 70% female. Therefore, women are more likely to negate biases associated with high-intensity primes.
3. The high-intensity prime we used (photo of a Muslim woman wearing a hijab) was, by coincidence, a topic in media narratives at the time of the study (see, for example, the quote attributed to Jeanine Pirro at the beginning of this chapter). Therefore, our high-intensity prime may have triggered negation responses from participant awareness that hijabs were targets of strong biases among some segments of the population.

These explanations—special populations and primes in current media contents—do not diminish the theoretical and practical significance of our study. We have shown that for special populations (college students and women) who may already be motivated to control their biases, strong primes can facilitate activation control. Similar findings are reported by Arendt (2013) for her college student sample. She showed activation control was facilitated by a series of semantic primes. We show that similar results can be observed for a high-intensity prime consisting of a single photograph. These results suggest that activation control intervention programs can work using high-intensity primes among populations already motivated to control biases. Two decades of research on implicit biases using the IAT have identified some of these populations: college students, women, and people who volunteer to take the IAT (almost all IAT takers are volunteers) (Nosek et al., 2007).

To improve external and internal validity of our study, we suggest recruiting a general population to participate, and increasing group sizes to at least 40 per group for stronger power and effect sizes. Whether general population participants will respond to strong primes as our college students did is a question meriting further study.

STUDY 2

Study 2 replicates Study 1 with three changes: first, instead of college students, participants are American adults. Second, we analyze stereotypes as predictors of behavioral intent. And third, we analyze whether political ideology mediates the relationship between primes, stereotypes, behavioral intent.

Using the same stimuli, measures of stereotypes, evaluations and behavioral intent, and experimental procedure as in Study 1, we ask the following research questions:

RQ1: What stereotypes of Muslim women applying for a university teaching job are activated by semantic (Muslim name) and visual (photos) primes? What stereotypes activate intent to hire?

RQ 2: What are the behavioral consequences of stereotypes: Which stereotypes predict intent to interview? Intent to hire?

RQ 3: Will a strong priming dose (photo of a Muslim woman in a hijab) activate stereotype control as indicated by more positive stereotypes and greater intent to hire, compared to lower doses (name, and a photo without the hijab)?

To refine our analysis, we introduce political ideology as a possible mediating variable of the relationship between priming dose and activation of stereotypes and behavioral intent. Political ideology—when conceptualized as degree of social conservatism and cognitive rigidity (Murphy & Hall, 2011)—predicts racial prejudice (Hodson & Busseri, 2012). Therefore, it is reasonable to expect that social conservatism (political ideology) will moderate activation control: social or political conservatives will be less likely to demonstrate activation control compared to social liberals. We seek answers to these questions in an online experiment with adult Americans recruited from an Amazon Mechanical Turk (MTurk) participant base.

Stereotypes are defined as "beliefs about the characteristics, attributes and behaviors of certain groups" (Hilton & von Hippel, 1996). Definition provided by Dovidio and Gaertner (1986) define stereotypes as "a collection of associations that link a target group to a set of descriptive characteristics" (p. 415). Finally, Hamilton and Troiler (1986, p.133) define stereotype as "a cognitive structure that contains the perceiver's knowledge, beliefs, and expectancies about some human group."

Ibroscheva and Ramaprasad (2008) argue that people are not born with stereotypes: stereotypes are acquired and are the product of cognition, simply—beliefs and attitudes. Moreover, stereotypes "assign identical characteristics to any person in a group, regardless of the actual variation among members of that group" (Aronson, 1988, p.332). Such generalization and categorization simplify the cognition of people and objects. As Tan (2021) explains, "it is easier to understand people within the characteristics and beliefs that already exist rather than evaluating individuals and objects" (p. 116). Stereotypes help people build the distinction between us and them, inside and outside groups. Stereotypes also facilitate the justification and explanation of people's behavior toward "them" (Stephan et al., 1993).

Stereotypes and Their Measures

Studies show that there is a number of ways to measure explicit stereotypes. For instance, Monteith and Spicer (2002) use free responses to measure White's and Black's racial attitudes. Other popular ways of measuring stereotypes are attribute checking (e.g., Katz & Braly, 1933), attribute ratings (e.g., Brigham, 1971), Group reality ratings (Tan, Fujioka, & Tan, 2000), and Belief scales (e.g., Barreto, Manzano, & Segura, 2012).

For the purpose of this study, we are using a semantic differential rating (e.g., Osgood et al., 1957; Gardner, 1973). Semantic differential rating allows to measure an object on an opposite adjective scale. In the case with stereotypes, the respondents are asked to check the space between two opposite adjectives. The closer the checked space to the adjective, the more likely this adjective is to be used to describe an object.

Stereotypes: Dimensions

Social perceptions of groups can be placed into two orthogonal dimensions— warmth and competence. Numerous studies define these two dimensions as fundamental for studies of social perceptions (e.g., Abele, Cuddy, Judd, & Yzerbyt, 2008; Cuddy, Fiske, & Glick, 2007; Fiske, Cuddy, Glick, & Xu, 2002; Fiske, Xu, Cuddy, & Glick, 1999).

Warmth and competence are embedded in the social content model (SCM) and, thus, allow to explain the impact of different structural variables on stereotypes as well as the impact of stereotypical content on attitudes and emotions toward different groups (Fiske et al., 1999, 2002). Warmth can be simply understood as the answer to the question, "What are this group's intentions?" while competence—"Is that group able to carry out its intentions?" (Kervyn, Fiske, & Yzerbyt, 2013).

Warmth is generally defined as "social desirability" and is linked to personal traits of sociability and likeability. Warmth can be measured by a Feeling Thermometer Scale (warm-cold), and by semantic differential adjectives such as warm/cold, pleasant/unpleasant; friendly/unfriendly; trustworthy/untrustworthy

(Sides & Gross, 2013). Competence, on the other hand, refers to how likely a group can accomplish goals. Competence is measured by semantic differential scales such as hardworking/lazy; intelligent/not intelligent; competent/not competent. In a study of stereotypes of Muslims and support for the "war on terror," Sides and Gross (2013) found that American adults had negative warmth stereotypes of Muslims, and less negative competence stereotypes. They also found that warmth stereotypes were stronger predictors of support for public policies supporting the War on Terror, compared to competence stereotypes.

Stereotypes of Muslims

Negative stereotypes of Muslims became dominant in the American society after the events of 9/11 (Sheridan, 2006). Americans link Muslims and Islam to terrorism, violence, extremism, and characterize them as culturally distinct, a threat to Western values (Kalkan, Layman, & Uslaner, 2009; Pew Research Center, 2014). Since 2015, stereotypes, prejudice, and discrimination toward Muslims became even worse, which is significantly explained by the vast spread of terrorist groups across the globe and the increased influence of ISIS (Brown, Ali, Stone, & Jewell, 2017).

Some studies portray Muslims as the ones lacking competence and intellectual sophistication (e.g., Viorst, 1994). Other studies show the portrayals of Muslims as somewhat competent and powerful. For instance, a depiction of Muslims with wealth (sheikhs) implicitly suggests a high societal status and consequently—power (Sides & Gross, 2013). Stereotypes of warmth, however, imply more negative portrayals of Muslims than the stereotypes of competence (e.g., Fiske et al., 2002).

Drawing on the 2004 ANES, Sides and Gross (2013) found a binary configuration of Muslim stereotypes. According to their findings, Muslims scored third lowest—closest to "very cold"—in a Feeling Thermometer Scale. Only gays and lesbians and illegal immigrants scored lower. Data from the 2006 and 2007 CCES indicate that random nationwide samples of American adults attributed the traits "hardworking," "intelligent," "violent," and "untrustworthy" to Muslims, a mixture of positive and negative stereotypes. Thus, Sides and Gross (2013) concluded that Muslim stereotypes consist of two dimensions: competence (hardworking and intelligent) and warmth (peaceful and trustworthy). American adults perceive Muslims to be competent but not warm.

These stereotypes, particularly the warmth dimension, direct evaluations and opinions. For example, respondents who rated Muslims low on the warmth dimension were the most likely to support public policies supporting the War on Terror such as decreased spending on foreign aid, increased spending on border security, and increased spending on the War on Terror (Sides & Gross, 2013).

Some studies also emphasize importance of differentiation between perceptions of Muslims and perceptions of Muslim Americans, as attitudes toward Muslim Americans are more favorable than attitudes toward Muslims from the Middle East (Nisbet, Ostman, & Shanahan, 2007; Traugott et al., 2002), disregarding the fact that attitudes toward both groups—Muslims and Muslim Americans—have common origins (Kalkan, Layman, & Uslaner, 2009). Even in the light of 9/11 events, the news coverage of Muslim Americans was overall more favorable to compare to the coverage of Muslims in general (e.g., Nacos & Torres-Reyna, 2003, 2007; Weston, 2003).

Political Ideology

Political ideology is generally defined as agreement or disagreement with socially conservative values. Social conservatism is indicated by resistance to change, desire to maintain existing social stratifications, a preference for "yes" or "no" answers, adherence to social conventions and traditions, a desire for "law and order," support for punitive punishment of "wrongdoers," and a desire for social control (Hodson & Busseri, 2012). There is consistent evidence that social conservatism predicts explicit and implicit racism (Keller, 2010; Murphy & Hall, 2011). Therefore, social conservatives might be more likely than social liberals to endorse negative stereotypes and less likely to demonstrate activation control.

Study 2 replicates the Tan, Vishnevskaya and Khan's (2019) college student study with a general adult population sample. Similar to the original study, we test the curvilinear relationship between prime dosage, negative stereotyping, and evaluations of a Muslim woman job applicant for a university teaching position, with the addition of political ideology, conceptualized as social conservatism, as a mediating variable. We also identify explicit stereotypes of Muslim women activated by the primes, and those stereotypes that predict intention to interview and intention to hire. In an online survey experiment with American adult participants, we test the following hypotheses:

H-1a: Compared to the low intensity prime (Muslim name), the moderate intensity prime (photo of Muslim woman) will be stereotyped and evaluated more negatively and will be less likely to be interviewed and hired.

H-1b: Compared to the moderate prime, the strong prime will be stereotyped and evaluated more negatively and will be less likely to be interviewed and hired.

H-2: Compared to the moderate prime, the strong prime (photo of a Muslim woman in a hijab) will be stereotyped and evaluated less negatively and will be more likely to be interviewed and hired.

H-1a and H-1b test priming theory: the stronger the prime, the more negative the stereotypes and behavioral intent. H-2 tests activation control theory: strong primes result in less negative stereotypes and behavioral intent.

Method

We used an online survey experiment with four levels of one factor. The factor is prime intensity. Based on theory and research on semantic and visual primes, and our discussion on Muslim women and clothing, the low-intensity prime is a typical Muslim woman's name; the moderate intensity prime is the Muslim name accompanied by a photograph of a Muslim woman; the high-intensity prime is the Muslim name accompanied by a photograph of the same Muslim woman wearing a hijab. We added a control condition using a name prime that is typically European American. Following previous studies on names and employment bias (e.g., Bertrand & Mullainathan, 2004; Rooth, 2010; Moss-Racusin et al., 2012), we recruited 200 adult Americans through MTurk to evaluate a job application for a university faculty position.

The application consisted of a CV. Dependent variables were stereotypes of Muslim women, evaluation of the applicant for the job, and behavioral intentions to hire.

Participants

Two hundred adult Americans were recruited to participate in the study through MTurk. MTurk is a cost-efficient way to collect survey data. It allows a higher generalizability of the findings as MTurk sample is representative of the population. Finally, despite the financial motivation to complete studies (in our case, participants were given $1 each as a reward for completed survey), studies show that MTurkers are more attentive to the provided instructions than other participants (e.g., college students), which makes MTurkers a reliable sample for social sciences' studies (see Hauser & Schwarz, 2016).

After cleaning the data, the final sample for the analysis consisted of 198 participants (105 males and 93 females). Racial distribution was 136 Whites, 35 Asians, 13 Latinos, 10 African Americans, and 3 mixed-race participants.

Study Design and Procedures

We used a randomized between-subject online experiment administered through two online survey platforms—Qualtrics and MTurk—with four conditions: control (Anglo-American woman's name); low-intensity prime (Muslim woman's name); moderate intensity prime (photo of a Muslim woman); and high-intensity prime (photo of a Muslim woman wearing a hijab).

The primes were accompanied by an identical resume for a teaching position at a university. We randomly assigned participants to one of the four conditions, resulting in 48–50 participants per group and presented the study to participants as an evaluation of a candidate for a faculty position at the university.

We instructed participants to read the position announcement and the applicant's CV before completing a questionnaire. Each group received only one condition—a CV with a European American name; a CV with a Muslim name; a CV with the Muslim name and a photo of the applicant without a hijab; and a CV with a Muslim name and a photo of the applicant with a hijab.

Participants completed the study online at their own time. We used Qualtrics to record questionnaire responses. The questionnaire itself was distributed through the MTurk platform. Participants were asked to provide a randomized four-digit code at the end of the survey. The code was also generated through Qualtrics. Once the completed surveys were recorded in Qualtrics, participants were paid $1 for participation.

The dependent variables were stereotypes of Muslim women (a semantic differential scale measuring warmth and competence), evaluations of the applicant for the faculty position (intent to interview), and intention to hire the applicant.

Stimulus Materials

The stimuli (factor levels) represented low, moderate, and high prime intensities plus a control condition without a Muslim prime. The low-intensity prime was a Muslim woman's name (Azhaar Basheera) accompanying the CV. The moderate prime was a photo accompanying the CV with the Muslim name. The high-intensity prime was a photo of the same woman wearing a hijab, accompanying the CV. This photo was identical to the photo used in Study 1. A veil covered the woman's head, hair, ears, and neck. The control condition was a CV with a European American name (Elizabeth Fitzgerald.) The CVs were identical in all conditions and included qualifications addressing position requirements in the announcement.

We chose the Muslim name from a directory of typical names for Muslim women (e.g., Sides & Gross, 2013); the European American name was from a directory of typical names for Irish American women. We selected the photo of the Muslim woman from a previous study, validating her facial features as typically Middle Eastern. The hijab was added by Photoshop.

Validation of our operationalization of prime intensity is provided by theories and studies reviewed earlier in this chapter. Visual primes such as photographs elicit stronger emotional and cognitive responses than semantic primes such as names. The hijab presents a strong visible sign of a "foreign" culture that contrasts with Western cultures.

Dependent Measures

We measured stereotypes of Muslim women, evaluations for the job, and behavioral intentions to hire as our dependent variables. For stereotypes, we used a 7-point semantic differential with nine bipolar adjectives representing "warmth" and "competence" dimensions adapted from Sides and Gross (2013). The warmth adjectives were warm/cold, friendly/not friendly, can be trusted/cannot be trusted, likable/not likable, and pleasant/not pleasant.

The competence adjectives were competent/not competent, hardworking/not hardworking, knowledgeable/not knowledgeable, articulate/not articulate. We added an overall evaluation: would be a good colleague/would not be a good colleague. To avoid response bias, we alternated positive and negative traits in the scales. We scored the ratings for each item from 1 (most negative) to 7 (most positive) and summed the item scores for all adjectives and separately for the warmth and competence dimensions.

We measured evaluations of the applicant for the job and intention to hire with questions adapted from Bertrand and Mullainathan (2004), Rooth (2010), and Moss-Racusin et al. (2012).

We summed up the scores separately for the evaluation items measuring warmth and competence, and for the behavioral items measuring intent to interview and intent to hire, from 1 (most negative response) to 5 (most positive response).

Analysis

To analyze data, we used SPSS software and performed four statistical analyses: MANOVA, ANOVA, confirmatory factor analysis, and standard multiple regression.

Results and Discussion

Participant Pool

Of the 200 respondents recruited from an MTurk pool, two were dropped because they did not complete the study in the allotted time. The remaining 198 participants were 105 males and 92 females; 136 Whites, 34 Asians, 13 Latinos, 10 African Americans, 1 Alaskan native, and 3 mixed race. Participants were assigned randomly to four experimental conditions.

We chose MTurk platform as MTurk participants are generally more educated, younger, and more computer literate than the general population (Clifford, Jewell, & Waggoner, 2015). In addition, MTurk participants, particularly self-identified "liberals," are more "open" than general public (Ibid.).

RQ1: Stereotypes of Muslim Women

The three Muslim primes—name, photo, photo with Hijab—consistently activated positive stereotypes, contrary to predictions from social learning theories, but consistent with activation control. Muslim women were perceived to be warm, friendly, trustworthy, pleasant, competent, hardworking, knowledgeable, and articulate across the four priming conditions. Few differences between conditions were found (see table 6.2).

Positive stereotyping across prime conditions can be explained by activation control theory. Even low and moderate primes motivated respondents to control implicit negative stereotypes, resulting in consistently positive stereotypes.

A factor analysis of the stereotype and other evaluative items produced three factors as the best solution. The dimensionality of the 11 items for evaluation of Muslim women was analyzed using principal component factor analysis. Laiser's criteria for eigenvalues greater than 1 were used to determine the number of factors. Three factors were rotated using oblimin rotation. The three factors explained 67.55% of the variance. They are Warmth/Competence, accounting for 40.29% of the variance; Qualification,

Table 6.2 Stereotypes of Muslim Women (Means Table)

Variables/Groups	Control	Low Prime	Moderate Prime	High Prime
Qualification	4.1739	4.06	3.9333	4.28
Interview	4.26	4.14	4.28	4.26
Hire	3.76	3.88	3.7556	3.98
Warm	4.826	5.040	5.467	4.78
Interact Student	4.00	3.98	4.1778	4.1
Interact Faculty	3.913**	4.1	4.1556	4.36**
Friendly	5.326	4.880**	5.60	5.82**
Trustworthy	5.522	5.5	5.444	5.46
Pleasant	5.478	4.7	5.556	5.4
Good Colleague	5.239	5.56	5.533	5.26
Competent	5.826	5.6	5.467	5.26
Hardworking	5.37	5.26	5.622	5.78
Knowledge	5.652	5.04	5.8	5.64
Articulate	5.391	5.42	5.489	5.76

*Group means differ on Tukey HSD at $p < 0.05$.
**Group means differ on both Tukey HSD and Scheffé both at $p < 0.05$.

16.32% of the variance, and Job Warmth, 8.775% of the variance. The three-factor solution indicates that perceptions of Muslim women clustered primarily as "warmth," consisting of stereotype traits indicating social closeness, competence, and expectations of positive interactions. "Qualifications" was a secondary factor. Therefore, when most people think of Muslim women, the primary question is, would I like this person to be a friend or colleague?

RQ2: Predictors of Intent to Interview, Intent to Hire

We used three standard multiple regression models to identify predictors of Intent to Interview and Intent to Hire.

In model 1, Intent to Hire was regressed onto Stereotype Warmth, Stereotype Competence, Prime Dosage (Experimental Groups 1, 2, 3, and 4) and Ideology (very conservative, conservative, neither conservative nor liberal, liberal, very liberal). The predictors explained 11% of the variance in Intent to Hire (F, 6, 19 = 3.952, p = 0.001). Only stereotype competence emerged as a significant predictor of Intent to Hire (B = 0.219, p = 0.04). With one standard deviation increase in stereotype competence, there is a 0.219 standard deviation increase in Intent to Hire. None of the other independent variables were significant predictors.

In model 2, Intent to Interview is the dependent variable. Independent variables are Stereotype Warmth, Stereotype Competence, Prime Dose, and Ideology. The predictors explained 14.7% of Intent to Interview (F, 6, 189 = 5.431, p < 0.001. Only Stereotype Competence significantly predicted Intent to Interview (B = 0.286, p = 0.007). With one standard deviation increase in stereotype competence, there is a 0.286 standard deviation increase in Intent to Interview.

In model 3, Intent to Hire is the dependent variable. Independent variables are Job Warmth, Qualification, Prime Dose, and Ideology. The predictors explained 47.7% of Intent to Hire (F, 6, 190 = 28.9, p < 0.001.) Job Warmth significantly predicted Intent to Hire (B = 0.188, p = 0.001). One standard deviation increase in Job Warmth led to a 0.185 standard deviation increase in Intent to Hire. Qualification was also a significant predictor (B = 0.613, p < 0.001). One standard deviation increase in Qualification led to a 0.613 standard deviation increase in Intent to Hire.

In model 4, Intent to Interview is the dependent variable; independent variables are Job Warmth, Qualification, Prime Dose, and Ideology. The predictors explained 35.6% of Intent to Interview (F, 6, 188 = 17.32, p < 0.001). Ideology significantly predicted Intent to Interview (B = 0.14, p = 0.02): the more liberal, the greater the Intent to Interview. One standard deviation increase in ideology led to a 0.14 standard deviation increase in

Intent to Interview. Qualification was also a significant predictor (B = 0.542, $p < 0.001$). With one standard deviation increase in Qualification, Intent to Interview increased by 0.542 standard deviations.

These regression models show that Competence and Qualification consistently predicted Intent to Interview and Intent to Hire, controlling for Warmth, Ideology, and Prime Dose. Although Muslim women were perceived to be both warm and competent, competence was the crucial variable. Our study participants, then, were acting "rationally": that is, they were not swayed in their behavioral intentions by liking or warmth, but instead based their intentions on perceptions of the job candidate's competence and qualifications.

RQ3 and Tests of Hypotheses: Effects of Prime Dose on Stereotypes

Our study tests hypotheses based on activation control theory. We predicted that stereotypes, Intent to Interview, and Intent to Hire would be most positive in the high prime condition, followed by low prime, and would be most negative in moderate prime. As Table 6.3 shows, a one-factor MANOVA test did not detect any significant differences between the prime groups.

The group means were consistently on the positive ends of the dependent variable scales and were not significantly different from each other and the control group (no prime). These results suggest that positive stereotypes were activated by all primes; even a low-dose prime (Muslim name) activated positive stereotypes, Intent to Interview, and Intent to Hire.

To test whether Ideology moderates the predicted activation control effects (activation control to be demonstrated by liberals and not by conservatives), we used two-way ANOVA with Ideology and Prime Dose as independent variables; stereotypes, Intent to Interview, and Intent to Hire were the dependent variables. The interaction between Ideology and Prime Dose was not significant. Prime dose did not significantly predict any of the dependent variables,

Table 6.3: Prime Dose by Stereotypes, Intent to Hire

Variables/Groups	Control Group	Low Prime	Moderate Prime	High Prime
	Table of Means			
Qualification	4.18	4.0769	3.9333	4.28
Stereotype Warmth	5.249	5.1558	5.52	5.344
Stereotype Competence	5.4983	5.3333	5.5944	5.61
Job Warmth	3.95	4.0577	4.1667	4.23
Intent to Hire	4.02	4.0192	4.0222	4.120

*Group means differ on both Tukey HSD and Scheffé test at $p < 0.05$.
**Group means differ using only Tukey HSD test at $p < 0.05$.

confirming results from the one-way ANOVA. Ideology significantly pre-dicted Stereotype Warmth (F, 2, 184 = 7.95), Stereotype Competence (F, 2, 184 = 5.25, $p<0.01$), and Intent to Interview (F, 2, 184 = 2.96, $p=0.054$), but not Intent to Hire. These results suggest that Ideology independently affects stereotypes and a behavioral intention.

Summary and Conclusions

Our study found:

1. Stereotypes of Muslim women in our participant pool are consistently positive, clustering as distinct "warmth" and "competence" dimensions.
2. Warmth explains most of the variance in the stereotype items.
3. Competence and Qualification are the strongest predictors of Intent to Interview and Intent to Hire.
4. Prime Dose did not affect stereotyping, Intent to Interview, and Intent to Hire. Positive stereotypes were activated in all prime conditions.
5. Ideology does not interact with Prime Dose in predicting stereotypes, Intent to Interview, and Intent to Hire.
6. Ideology independently predicts Stereotype Warmth, Stereotype Competence, and Intent to Interview.

These results suggest that among educated, computer-literate people (MTurk participant pool), primes that signal the identity of a marginal-ized group (Muslim women) can activate control of negative evaluations, resulting in positive stereotypes and behavioral intentions. These results are similar to studies of activation control among judges (Rachilinski, Johnson, Wistrich, & Guthrie, 2009) and college students (Tan, Vishnevskaya, & Khan, 2019).

Even minimal primes such as a name, can elicit activation control effects. Prime strength is not a factor—a name, a photo, and a photo with group identifying cues (hijab) produce similar results—positive evaluations of a stigmatized group. This finding can be explained by motivation among certain segments of American society to be fair and unbiased in their interactions with "other" groups. This motivation is heightened by negative discourse, signals, and symbols in the environment such as media portrayals and state-ments from public officials: the more negative the discourse, the greater the motivation to control negative evaluations, and therefore the more positive the stereotypes and behavioral intentions. Whether this motivation to control biases can be observed in more conservative segments of the population is open to question.

Our study shows that conservative ideology leads to less positive evaluations of Muslim women, suggesting that in this group, primes may elicit in a linear fashion, increasingly negative evaluations of stigmatized groups. For Muslim women, the effects of primes in contexts other than a university teaching position can be studied. For example, can Muslim identifiers (primes) influence perceptions about the suitability of Muslim women for public office? Some recent public rhetoric (Soltani, 2016: "Go back to where you came from"; "Wrap that towel around her neck"; "Time for target practice") may activate stereotype control among socially liberal voters, and reinforcement of stereotypes among conservative voters. These questions can be investigated in future research.

STUDY 3

Study 3 refines analysis of priming and activation control in Studies 1 and 2 by confining the experiment to weak, moderate, and strong primes, analyzing only White adult Americans, and by further looking at political ideology as a mediator. Studies 1 and 2 provide evidence of activation control rather than priming. In Study 3, we analyze weak (Muslim woman without hijab), moderate (Muslim woman with hijab covering the head only), and strong (Muslim woman with hijab covering her head and part of her face) primes to make comparisons based on strength of prime only, rather than including a control (Western name) and a very weak (Muslim name) primes, which Studies 1 and 2 have shown to have no influence on either priming or activation. Activation occurred with the strongest prime (woman with hijab) compared to a weak prime (woman without hijab.) So, the addition of a stronger prime allows us to test whether activation is a function of prime strength. Similarly, Sheen et al. (2018) used only moderate, strong and very strong primes (photos of Muslim women), eliminating control and weak primes, in their study of the effects of wearing the hijab on perceived facial attractiveness.

Most studies of anti-Muslim bias use White samples because anti-Muslim aggressions in the world are committed by Whites (young White men) (Ciftci, 2012). In studies using the IAT and explicit measures, Hispanics and Jews show the least anti-Muslim bias; White fundamentalist Christians showed the most bias. Therefore, we are interested in whether activation control is demonstrated by White Americans, a group most likely to be biased against Muslims compared to other racial groups in the United States.

Studies in the United States and the United Kingdom have identified differences in how self-identified conservatives and liberals process information and their social environments. Conservatives are more likely than liberals to prefer "Yes" or "No" answers; are more resistant to information contradicting existing beliefs; are more likely to consider out-groups such as immigrants as threats; are more likely to prefer the status quo over change; and are less likely to have personal contact with out-group members (Jost et al., 2003). Conservatives are also more likely than liberals to be implicitly and explicitly biased against out-groups, including the endorsement of negative stereotypes and discriminatory practices (Stankov, 2009). Therefore, conservatives may be less likely than liberals to control the activation of negative stereotypes and their application.

In Study 3, we ask the following research questions:

RQ1: Is activation control of anti-Muslim women stereotypes and behavioral intent a function of prime strength? That, is will activation control be strongest in the strong prime condition compared to the moderate and weak prime conditions?

RQ2: Will activation control be demonstrated by liberals more strongly compared to conservatives?

These research questions lead to the following hypotheses:

H-1: Compared to weak and moderate primes, the strong prime will be stereotyped less negatively and will be more likely to be interviewed and hired.
    H-1 is a test of a main effect of strength of prime across liberal and conservative participants.

H-2: For liberals, the strong prime will be stereotyped less negatively and will be more likely interviewed and hired compared to weak and moderate primes. For liberals, stereotyping and intent to hire and interview will not be affected by prime strength: stereotyping and intent to interview/hire will be equal among weak, moderate, and strong prime participants.
    H-2 is a test of interaction between prime strength and ideology. Activation control occurs for liberals, but not for conservatives.

Participants

As in Study 2, we recruited participants from MTurk, a common source of samples of adult Americans. MTurk participants are more educated, more liberal, and more knowledgeable about technology than the average American. However, they provide more representative samples than those provided by social media and other online sources (Hauser & Schwarz, 2016). Also, in an experiment such as ours, extraneous variance from demographic and other environmental factors can be controlled by random assignment to conditions.

Out of an original pool of 400 participants, we identified 273 (66.6%) who identified as White. Dropped from the analysis were Black or African Americans (7.8%), Asians (17.1%), Native Hawaiian or other Pacific Islanders (0.2%), and Hispanics (7.3%).

For political ideology, we identified 76 White respondents who self-identified as conservative or very conservative, and 68 White respondents who self-identified as liberal or very liberal.

Respondents who did not answer at least one question in the experiment (missing values) were dropped from the analysis, resulting in a total N of 144, 76 White conservatives and 68 White liberals.

Experimental Design and Procedure

We used a 3 (prime strength: weak, moderate, strong) by 2 (political ideology: conservative, liberal) randomized between-subjects' factorial design. Liberals and conservatives were randomly assigned to one of the prime conditions, resulting in cell sizes of 23 to 27.

As in Studies 1 and 2, we instructed the participants to read the position announcement and the CV (identical for all conditions). Each group received only one condition: a CV with a photo of the applicant, a Muslim woman (weak prime); a CV with a photo of a Muslim woman in a hijab covering her head (moderate prime); a CV with a photo of a Muslim woman in a hijab covering her head and part of her face (strong prime). The CVs and job announcement were identical in all conditions and were identical to those used in Studies 1 and 2. The only difference between conditions was the photo of the Muslim woman.

We told participants that we were asking them to help evaluate an applicant for a teaching position at a public university. We instructed them to read the position announcement and the applicant's CV. We then asked them to complete a questionnaire which measured our dependent variables (discussed below).

Participants completed the study online at their own time. We used Qualtrics to record questionnaire responses which was distributed through the MTurk platform. Participants provided a randomized four-digit code at the end of the survey. Once the completed surveys were recorded in Qualtrics, they were paid $1 for participation.

Stimulus Materials (Primes)

To prime stereotypes of Muslim women, we used three photos attached to identical CVs. The weak prime was a head shot of a Muslim woman. The moderate prime was a head shot of a Muslim woman wearing a hijab that covered her head. The strong prime was a head shot of the Muslim woman in the moderate prime but wearing a hijab that covered her head and part of her face. The woman in the weak prime was judged by three graduate students as similar in attractiveness to the woman in the moderate and strong prime photographs. Three graduate students judged the photo of the woman with the hijab covering her head to be less identifiable as a devout Muslim compared to the woman with the hijab covering her head and face. Our stimuli representing weak (no hijab), moderate, and strong primes are confirmed in other studies of primes and stereotype activation (Sheen et al., 2018).

The weak prime was a head shot of a Muslim woman, the same photo used in Studies 1 and 2. The moderate prime was a head shot of a Muslim woman wearing a hijab that covered her head, hair, ears, and neck. The strong prime was a head shot of the Muslim woman in the moderate prime wearing a hijab that covered her head, forehead, ears, and hair. The strong prime photo also showed the woman's shoulders and upper arms covered by a burqa. Three graduate students judged the moderate prime woman to be less identifiable as a devout Muslim than the strong prime woman.

Dependent Variables

Behavioral Intent

We used four items to measure behavioral intent to hire: How qualified is the candidate; Invite to campus for an interview; would you hire; how well would the candidate interact with students; interact with other faculty. Responses were on a 5-point scale, with 5 the most positive response, 1 the most negative. An exploratory factor analysis, principal components with orthogonal rotation produced two factors: Intent to hire (qualified, interview, hire) and Interaction (interact with students, faculty). Mean scores for items in each factor were aggregated into a factor mean and used in the analysis.

Stereotypes

We used a 7-point semantic differential to measure stereotypes, scored from 1 (positive) to 5 (negative). The adjectives were "can be trusted/can't be trusted"; "friendly/not friendly"; "articulate/not articulate"; "active/passive"; "can act independently/cannot act independently"; "Would fit in/would not fit in"; "can lead change/cannot lead change"; "can adapt to change/cannot adapt to change"; "would be a good colleague/would not be a good colleague." We chose these descriptors from negative stereotypes of Muslim women identified in previous studies (Bertrand & Mullainathan, 2004; Rooth, 2010; Moss-Racusin et al., 2012). The ten semantic differential descriptors loaded on one factor, which we labeled "affective" evaluations. Mean scores for the ten semantic differential items were aggregated into a factor mean and used in the analysis.

Analysis

We used two-way ANOVA to test for main effects (prime; ideology) and interaction (prime*ideology) on each of the dependent variables: Intent to Hire; Interaction with Students and Faculty; Affective evaluations (semantic differential). We looked for significant effects at $p=/<0.05$ but did not rely only on significance tests to interpret results. We also looked at plot profiles to evaluate interaction effects, a strategy recommended by a growing number of statisticians. For example, Wasserstein et al. (2019) recommends "moving to a world beyond $p<.05$." An issue of *The American Statistician* (2019) features 41 articles providing evidence to support less reliance on p values and using other evidence to interpret results particularly when theories provide strong foundations for the predictions and when cell sizes are small (Wasserstein et al., 2019). Both conditions are found in our Study 3. Theory and previous research support activation control hypotheses. Our cell sizes range from 23 to 27. G-power analysis suggests that we would need an N of 52 per group to find a large effect size (Cohen's $d=0.8$ or larger) at 80% power. Our cell sizes were relatively smaller because we included in the analysis a second factor (political ideology).

Results

Intent to Hire

Main effects for prime and ideology on Intent to Hire were not significant at $p=0.05$. Interaction between prime and ideology was also not significant. Observed power for the corrected model was 0.189 or approaching a "small effect" (Cohen, 1988).

Figure 6.1 shows a possible activation effect for liberals, and a possible priming effect for conservatives. For liberals, ratings increased and were the most positive with the strong prime. For conservatives, ratings decreased and were the most negative with the strong prime. It's possible that liberals were cued by the photo of the applicant in a hijab covering the head and face to control implicit biases and therefore self-corrected by assigning higher ratings to the applicant. For conservatives, the strong prime activated negative biases which they did not control, resulting in the lowest ratings of the applicant.

Interactions with Students and Faculty

Main effects for prime and ideology on Faculty/Student Interactions were not significant. Observed power for the corrected model was 0.507, a medium

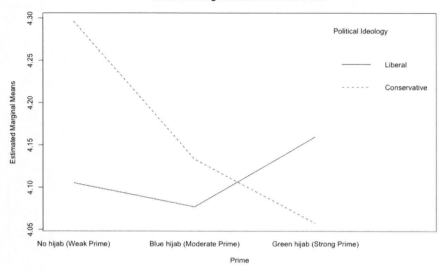

Figure 6.1   Estimated Marginal Means of Intent to Hire. *Source*: Created by authors.

effect (Cohen, 1988). Figure 6.2 shows a possible priming effect for conservatives and a possible activation effect for both liberals and conservatives. For conservatives, the most negative ratings (high score) were activated by the moderate prime, a steep increase from the weak prime, indicating that even a moderate prime can activate negative perceptions, a trend that was not evident for liberals. For liberals and conservatives, the most positive ratings (low scores) were in the strong prime condition, indicating that both liberals and conservatives self-corrected when cued by a strong prime. Liberals showed a steeper increase in positive ratings in the strong prime conditions from the moderate prime condition. These results indicate that conservatives are more likely than liberals to activate negative biases when presented with even moderate primes. Liberals and conservatives self-corrected negative biases when presented with strong primes, an activation control response.

Affective Evaluation (Semantic Differential)

Main effects on affective evaluations were significant for primes (p=0.018) and ideology (p=0.001). The interaction between prime and ideology was not significant. The corrected model was significant at $p = 0.005$. Observed power was large for the corrected model (0.87), prime (0.627), and ideology (0.844). As figure 6.3 shows, liberals rated the applicant more positively (positive rating = lower score) than conservatives across all prime conditions. Ratings

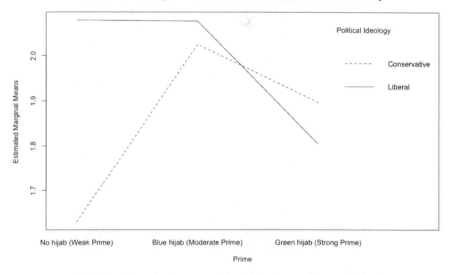

Figure 6.2   Estimated Marginal Means of Interactions with Students and Faculty.
Source: Created by authors.

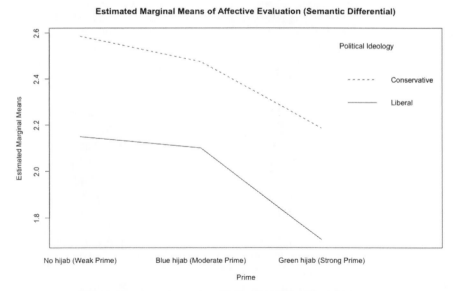

Figure 6.3   Estimated Marginal Means of Affective Evaluation (Semantic Differential).
Source: Created by authors.

for both liberals and conservatives dipped (became more positive) from the weak to moderate to strong prime conditions, with the most positive (lowest scores) ratings in the strong prime condition. Liberals and conservatives corrected negative evaluations activated by the weak and moderate primes when presented with a strong prime. The woman in a hijab covering head and face appears to have motivated liberals and conservatives to control application of negative stereotypes.

Conclusions

Study 3 suggests that analysis of priming and activation effects should consider ideology and whether behavioral intent or affective evaluations are the dependent variable. For a direct behavioral intent response to primes, liberals show activation control: the stronger the prime, the more positive the response. Conservatives, on the other hand, show a priming response: the stronger the prime, the more negative evaluation. As a post hoc explanation, the strong prime condition (Muslim woman in a hijab covering the head and face) was seen as a threat by conservatives, and therefore was evaluated more negatively. Behavioral intent was operationalized in the study as a highly personalized evaluation ("Would you invite for an interview; Would you hire?") and therefore represented a personal commitment. Liberals, on the other hand, were motivated by the high prime to control negative evaluations from negative stereotyping. Instead of seeing the Muslim woman as a threat, she reminded them that stereotypes should not be used as a basis for a behavioral evaluation or commitment. Therefore, they evaluated her more positively compared to the moderate prime.

Expected interactions between faculty and students, while still a behavioral intent, were less of a personal decision than commitment to hire. Results of expected interactions show that among conservatives, the moderate prime activated negative evaluations, and the strong prime activated control of negative evaluations. Liberals did not demonstrate priming effects. Instead, they showed activation control by rating the applicant most positively in the strong prime condition. With behavioral intent that is less personal, liberals and conservatives showed activation control with a strong prime; conservatives showed a priming effect with a moderate prime.

Affective evaluations generally do not require a personal commitment. Evaluating a person on a semantic differential does not imply a commitment to interact with that person. Therefore, it takes less effort to control negative affective evaluations. In Study 3, both liberals and conservatives demonstrated activation control. While liberals rated the applicant more positively than conservatives on the semantic differential, the most positive evaluations were in the strong prime condition. One explanation is that participants in the strong prime condition were controlling the use of a generalized negative impression initially activated by the photo, by rating the applicant more positively in the semantic differential.

While we did not test most of these explanations in our study, they are suggested by theory and previous research (Rudman, Ashmore & Gary, 2001). Responses of people to hypothetical situations as those posed in most research questionnaires depend not only on the experimental inductions but on the degree of personal commitment called for in the responses. Liberals and conservatives respond differently to some of these hypothetical situations because of differences in how they process the environment, other people, and information.

SUMMARY AND CONCLUSIONS: STUDIES 1, 2, AND 3

Results from Studies 1, 2, and 3 are consistent and supportive of each other. Study 1 found support for activation control of stereotype use among college students. A single dose of a strong (moderate in Study 3) prime (a photograph of a Muslim woman wearing a hijab) resulted in the most positive stereotypes and evaluations of a Muslim woman job applicant, particularly for the warmth dimension. Study 1 did not support predictions from cultivation and social learning theories. Stereotypes and evaluations did not become more negative as prime intensity increase. Strong primes activated stereotype use and control; they did not activate negative evaluations.

Study 2 showed that among American adults, moderate (Muslim name) and strong (Muslim woman wearing a hijab) activate control of negative evaluations, resulting in positive stereotypes and behavioral intentions. Prime strength is not a factor. Even a minimal (weak) prime activated stereotype application control and resulted in positive evaluations of the job applicant. Perceived competence and qualifications of the candidate were the strongest predictors of intent to interview and hire, suggesting that participants were attempting to base decisions on "rational" criteria rather than implicit biases initially activated by the primes. Ideology independently predicted stereotype warmth, stereotype competence, and intent to interview: Conservatives were more likely than liberals to evaluate the job applicant negatively.

Study 3 analyzed three levels of primes: weak (Muslim woman without a hijab), moderate (Muslim woman in a hijab covering her head), and strong (Muslim woman in a hijab covering her head and face). The strong prime was not used in Studies 1 and 2. Also, we analyzed ideology as a two-level factor (conservatives and liberals). Participants were American adults. Study 3 found that liberals controlled negative biases for behavioral intent to hire and interview, a demonstration of activation control. Conservatives, on the other hand, expressed more negative behavioral intentions with the strong prime, an indication of priming. For evaluations of interactions with students and faculty, liberals showed activation control: the strong prime resulted in the most positive evaluations. Conservatives gave the most negative ratings of the job applicant in the moderate prime condition, an indication of priming effects. However, conservatives demonstrated activation control (more positive evaluations) in the strong prime condition. Therefore, both liberals and conservatives showed activation control. Priming of negative evaluations occurred with the moderate prime, but only among conservatives.

For affective evaluations such as those measured by the semantic differential that do not directly imply anticipated behaviors, both conservatives and liberals demonstrate activation control. The strong prime, compared to weak and moderate primes, elicited the most positive evaluations.

Studies 1, 2, and 3 provide evidence of activation control among educated participants and among participants who self-identify as liberals. This finding is more evident for measures of behavioral intent compared to affective measures such as stereotypes.

Theory and other research support these conclusions. Studies 1 and 2 relied exclusively on tests of significance. Results from Study 3 were interpreted based on F-tests and profile plots rather than on significance tests exclusively.

Implications of our findings for practical use in mitigating the effects of anti-Muslim women bias are discussed in chapters 7 (Interventions Applied to Muslim Women) and 8 (Conclusions and Recommendations) of this book.

APPENDIX A: EXPERIMENTAL PROTOCOL

Instructions to Participants

Thank you for participating in this exercise. The purpose is to evaluate an applicant for an instructor position in XXXXXXX. You will receive extra credit points for participating. Participation is voluntary. Please read the job description below, the applicant's CV, and complete the questionnaire that follows. Your responses are anonymous. You will not be identified in the questionnaire. Responses will be analyzed in the aggregate by group.

Job Description

Title: Instructor, XXXXXXXXXXX
Terms of appointment: Nine-month renewable appointment with summer teaching possible depending on student enrollment. Competitive salary.

Duties: Teach 4 classes per semester in Public Speaking or Communication and Society. Advise and mentor students. Participate in college committees.

Minimum requirements: an MA in Communication or related field; experience in teaching undergraduate college students; ability to communicate effectively, verbally, and in writing complex communication concepts to college undergraduates; ability to relate and communicate with undergraduate students at XXXXXXXX

Curriculum Vitae of the Applicant

Bachelor of Arts, Communication, XXXXXXXXX university.

Master of Arts, Communication, XXXXX university

MA Thesis: Visual Images in Corporate Advertising and Consumer Responses

Teaching Experience: Teaching assistant, XXXXX: assisted senior faculty in teaching, beginning undergraduate courses in Communication and Society, Strategic Communication and New Media (2016–2018)

Awards: Teaching Assistantship, XXXX; best student paper, Media and Society division, International Communication Association conference, XXXXX 2018.

Professional Experience: Student Intern (XXXXXX a public-relations firm, summer, 2016.) References: available upon request

NOTE

1. Discussed more thoroughly in chapter 4: Priming and Activation Control of Stereotypes

Chapter 7

Interventions Applied
to Muslim Women

Driven by concerns for the victimization of Muslims in general and Muslim women in particular, researchers have turned their attention to best practices and strategies that can reduce and control the frequency and effects of Islamophobic hate crimes and aggressions. These interventions address under-reporting of aggressions, intra-personal or individual strategies to prevent the activation of stereotypes, and media narratives and primes to prevent stereotype activation.

INCREASING REPORTING OF AGGRESSIONS:
COMMUNITY SUPPORT

Most Americans (up to 70%) admit that they know very little about Muslims; only about 38% say they know someone who is Muslim (Pew Research Center, 2017; Institute for Social Policy and Understanding, 2021). Muslims accurately perceive that most Americans including law-enforcement officers do not understand them. As a consequence, there is general distrust and reluctance to report hate crimes and other acts of aggression.

Accurate reporting of Islamophobic aggressions and hate crimes facilitate prosecutions and public awareness. To increase accuracy, community-based third-party reporting agencies have been established in communities across the United States and Europe. Muslim communities have organized agencies and identified people who can be trusted by victims and who have working knowledge of Islam and the culture of victims. Victims will be respected, will feel that they are taken seriously, and will be assured that their reporting of aggressions will make a difference. These community organizations provide accessible reporting channels such as social media and other online platforms.

They ensure that the reports will be included in public records such as FBI and police reports. They facilitate the prosecution of hate crimes. In doing so, these community organizations promote public and media awareness and action by policy makers.

A good model is the British organization Measuring Anti-Muslim Attacks or "MAMA," a nationwide organization that provides victims of Islamophobic hate crimes and aggressions in the United Kingdom an opportunity to report and provide details of Islamophobic aggressions. Victims can speak to trained staff by free phones or report by email, SMS, Twitter, Facebook, and the MAMA website. Most of the victims are Muslim women (Allen, 2015).

In the United States, nonprofit organizations such as the Gamaliel Foundation and the Industrial Areas Foundation (IAF) provide community services and develop coalitions across racial and religious groups to counter Islamophobia. The Institute for Social Policy and Understanding (ISPU) conducts scientific research and provides information to the general public, the media, and policymakers about American Muslims. Although these organizations do not specifically provide reporting mechanisms, they are influential advocates for American Muslims and are credible and trustworthy sources of information.

INTRAPERSONAL INTERVENTIONS TO PREVENT ACTIVATION OF ANTI-MUSLIM STEREOTYPES

Intrapersonal interventions for preventing the activation of negative stereotypes toward Muslim women are based on interventions for reducing the activation of negative stereotypes of marginalized groups in general such as racial minorities. Intrapersonal interventions fall into two categories: control of stereotype activation so that they are not activated at all; and control of stereotype use, so that activated stereotypes do not negatively influence evaluations of and behaviors toward the targeted group (Moskowitz & Stone, 2012). These interventions are intrapersonal: they involve introspection and motivation initiated by the individual.

Controlling Stereotype Activation

To prevent stereotype activation, intrapersonal interventions focus on goals for interaction with the target group; personal assessments of self-worth and values; and redefining the salience or relevance of the targeted individual's group. These interventions are proactive. They require, first, realization and acceptance by the perceiver that stereotypes may be activated in a particular interaction, and second, a willingness to engage in the intervention.

These requirements for stereotype activation control are not unreasonable, considering that most Americans who hold implicit biases are also willing to control stereotyping that leads to those biases (Nosek et al., 2011.) With information on how to control the activation of stereotypes, we can assume that they will proactively use these interventions.

Goals

Stereotypes help the individual adapt to the environment and provide meaning to and validation of the self. Stereotypes provide a summary evaluation of other people based on group membership. In most cultures, people have generalized perceptions of groups based on early socialization, information from the media, and personal experiences. Research has established that these cultural stereotypes are based on incomplete and inaccurate information. They provide a heuristic, easy, low-effort strategy for making sense of other people (Gilbert & Hixon, 1991). Cultural stereotypes are activated when the perceiver is exposed to primes, most simply a member of the targeted group. According to experimental studies, activation of cultural stereotypes is prevented when the perceiver is made aware by a third party such as by another person or an information medium of inaccuracies in stereotyping. A prime such as a cartoon exaggerating stereotypical physical features of a target person can remind the perceiver that stereotypes are inaccurate representations of reality, and that sense-making requires attention to a full range of information available in the present encounter (Moskowitz & Stone, 2012). Conscious altering of a goal from simple sense-making to avoiding stereotyping can prevent stereotype activation.

Personal Assessment of Self-Worth

Experimental studies have shown that negative stereotypes are more likely to be activated when people are angry and when their self-worth has been challenged (Moskowitz & Stone, 2012). In some of these studies, manipulations include giving a "test" to participants. Half are told that they did well; the other half that they did not do well. Activation of negative stereotypes toward an out-group such as racial minority is more likely when participants are told they did not do well and when the test is presented as an evaluation of a trait or ability important to them such as cognitive ability. In the experiments, self-worth was lowered by the bogus test results. Stereotype activation, mostly disparaging of an out-group, fulfilled a function of stereotyping—restoration of self-esteem. Reminders that out-groups such as Muslims are not threats, and reminders that the identities of in-groups are of value in the community can prevent threats to estimations of self-worth and therefore prevent stereotype activation. Reminders can be media narratives or primes.

Personal Assessment of Values

Most Americans profess to egalitarian values such as equality. Surveys have shown that these values are often ranked second only to freedom in importance (Ball-Rokeach et al., 1984). When people are reminded that egalitarian values are important not only to the self but to the community, stereotype activation can be prevented. Reminders of egalitarian values can be accomplished through self-assessment and by the media. Narratives that explicitly promote egalitarian values can be effective reminders. Most negative stereotypes contradict egalitarian values. The assignment of summary negative traits and behaviors to out-groups promote unequal treatment. A person who professes to be egalitarian will be in a state of mental and emotional discomfort or cognitive dissonance (Festinger, 1978) when he/she activates a negative stereotype of an out-group. Therefore, he/she will be motivated to avoid stereotyping.

Re-Definition of Categories

Members of out-groups belong to several categories based on race, ethnicity, religion, gender, age, employment, income, education, and other demographic characteristics. In the United States, race, ethnicity, and religion are often used to negatively stereotype out-groups. These categories provide simplistic criteria for "us' versus "them" differentiations. Physical characteristics (e.g., skin tone) and dress (e.g., hijab) instantly identify group members as the "other." Negative stereotypes are activated by visible identifiers. Most negative stereotypes ignore traits that can be associated with other groups besides race or religion that the out-group member may belong to. Studies have shown that people are less likely to activate negative stereotypes they associate with perceived primary group membership of the target person (e.g., race) when they are reminded of another target group category that is more salient to the present situation. The perceiver can then consciously or unconsciously re-categorize the target person into another group. Re-categorization can be accomplished by narratives displaying the wide range of experiences of target persons based on multiple identities or group memberships, and simply, by primes. One study found that a video showing a Chinese woman putting on lipstick activated stereotypes of women and not of Chinese people. A video showing a Chinese woman using chopsticks activated Chinese, and not female stereotypes (Macrae et al., 1995). Similarly, a photo of a Muslim woman with a hijab dressed as a medical doctor will activate stereotypes that are different from stereotypes that might be activated by a photo of the same Muslim woman in a burqa in the ruins of bombed building in a war zone.

Application to Muslim Women

Applied to Muslim women, Americans can be reminded through self-introspection in schools and by primes and narratives in the media that stereotyping leads to inaccurate assessments of people, Muslim women in particular; that Muslim women are not a threat to American society; that egalitarian values apply to Muslim women; and that Muslim women are doctors, lawyers, accountants, teachers, are highly educated; and that they are Americans. The Pew Research Center (2017) and the Institute for Policy and Understanding (2021) provide useful, objective information.

Challenges to Preventing Activation of Stereotypes

Although interventions to activation control of stereotypes have been identified in laboratory experiments, their application in the real world needs further study. The interventions require conscious motivation of perceivers. Most stereotypes, including stereotypes of Muslim women, are implicitly rather than explicitly held; their activation is unconscious, automatic, and spontaneous, yet activation control is a conscious strategy. Whether the interventions in laboratory studies that induce conscious strategies apply in the real world remains to be studied. Because of this uncertainty, recent research has focused on identifying effective interventions to control the use of stereotypes once they have been activated (FitzGerald et al., 2019).

INTRAPERSONAL INTERVENTIONS TO PREVENT ACTIVATION OF USE OF ANTI-MUSLIM STEREOTYPES

Once stereotypes are activated, their use can be controlled through conscious effort. These interventions are under the conscious control of the perceiver and require motivation to apply them. The assumption is that most people can be made aware when negative stereotyping has been activated and will be motivated to control the use of those stereotypes in biased evaluations and behaviors. This process has been documented among judges, physicians, teachers, and the general public (Tan, 2021).

In a review of 30 studies between 2005 and 2015, FitzGerald, Martin, Berner, and Hurst (2019) identified several interventions that can prevent activation of stereotype application. Some of these interventions are similar to those that work to prevent stereotype activation. The difference is that these strategies are consciously used by perceivers to control use or application once stereotypes are activated.

1. Perspective taking. Taking the perspective of the out-group member promotes empathy. How does the targeted person feel about being negatively stereotyped and discriminated against, Perspective taking is accomplished, in studies, by having research participants write from the viewpoint of a targeted person who is the object of prejudice (e.g., victim of aggression, profiled); reading first-person experiences by targeted group members; imagining positive personal interactions with an out-group member; reading or seeing narratives in the media about targeted out-group members. Most studies show that focusing on emotions (how the targeted person felt) works better than focusing on facts and information.

2. Identification with the out-group. Participants are taught or encouraged to identify common categories with the out-group (e.g., women; teachers; students) and to look for similarities rather than differences. This can be accomplished by priming and narratives that promote common categories (e.g., Americans), and by personal contact with the out-group. Personal contact promotes identification and individuation. Target persons are seen as individuals who transcend previously assigned stereotypes.

3. Exposure to counter-stereotypical exemplars. These are examples from the targeted group who counter prevailing stereotypes; for example, a Muslim woman who is a physician; a woman who is a corporate executive; an Asian American who is a general in the military. Counter-stereotypes can be promoted in primes (photos; words) and narratives (success stories) in the media.

4. Appeal to egalitarian values. As with control of stereotype activation, reinforcement of equality can remind people not to discriminate against persons targeted by negative stereotypes. These appeals can be repeated in the media and in interpersonal communication in-person or in social media.

5. Evaluative conditioning. Participants are trained and educated to control stereotype use generally, and specifically, to apply counter-stereotypes to the targeted group. This can be accomplished in the media and schools, and at an individual level, through imagination. Imagining counter-stereotypes (e.g., a strong woman) prevents use of negative stereotyping in discriminatory evaluations and behaviors.

6. Inducing emotions. Studies have shown that research participants who are in a "good mood" are less likely to apply negative stereotypes compared to participants who are angry or frustrated. Positive emotions can be induced by "feel good" narratives featuring targeted group members.

These interventions work in experiments in varying degrees of effectiveness. The most effective, supported in a number of studies, are counter-stereotypical exemplars (FitzGerald et al., 2019). It's unclear whether these interventions work in the real world. Theoretically, they should work, but the difficulty in applying them in field studies remains a challenge. For the moment, based on decades of experimental research, we'll assume they can work.

Application to Muslim Women

Applied to Muslim women, interventions likely to be effective in controlling application of negative stereotypes are narratives and primes promoting counter-stereotypical exemplars of Muslim women in a wide range of activities, careers, and roles; and emotional appeals focusing on how Muslim women feel as targets of prejudicial attitudes and behaviors. In general, rational appeals such as data on education and careers do not work as well as emotional appeals. Many of these interventions require external support for the perceiver. A primary source of support are the media—news and entertainment in television, newspapers, and social media.

MEDIA INTERVENTIONS

Large majorities of Americans admit they know very little or little about Muslims, and only a small minority (38%) say they know someone who is a Muslim (Pew Research Center, 2017; ISPU, 2021). Yet, majorities express prejudicial attitudes and negative stereotypes about Muslims (chapter 2, this book).

National surveys show that television and newspapers are the main sources of information about Muslims. A conclusion, then, is that Muslim biases are held by the informed. What information used is often from the media (television primarily) and from conversations with like-minded people in social media (Pew Research Center, 2017). National surveys have shown that television and newspapers are the main sources of information about Muslims. The most frequently mentioned influence on public attitudes about Muslims in the United States is "the media" (48%) (Pew Research Center, 2017; Cashin, 2010). Experimental studies have shown that even brief exposure to media contents influence perceptions of Muslims and other minorities: positive primes and narratives lead to positive stereotypes and liking while negative contents lead to negative stereotypes and disliking (Johnson, 2014). Considering that most media portrayals of Muslims are negative rather than realistic (chapter 3), media interventions should address this imbalance.

Online conspiracy theories have aided the spread of misinformation about Muslims to instigate fear and hatred in the United States and abroad (Human Rights Council, 2019). Around the world, conspiracy theories include the lie that immigrant Muslim populations are going to "outbreed" native populations; that Muslim men conspire to seduce non-Muslim women into converting to Islam; and that Muslims are deliberately conspiring to spread COVID 19 (Human Rights Council, 2019). In the United States, a conspiracy popular among White supremacist groups is "Sharia panic" which claims that American Muslims are undermining the American constitution and trying to overthrow the US government by implementing "Shariah religious law" in legal proceeding in the country (Salon.com, 2015). According to this false conspiracy theory, "Sharia law" will place American women at risk of subjugation by Muslim men. Another right-wing conspiracy theory is that there are up to 35 secret Muslim terrorist training camps in rural areas of the United States, reinforcing stereotypes of Muslims as terrorists' intent on overthrowing the US government (Salon.com, 2015). These online lies gain traction when legitimate mainstream media report them and when they become a focus of online chatter. Even when labeled as "false conspiracy theories," images and words (e.g., "terrorist camps") imbedded in reports are primes that activate latent biases against Muslims.

Interventions to control the activation of stereotypes of Muslim women and the application of these stereotypes should address portrayals in the media. For media interventions to be effective, media professionals—reporters, writers, editors, producers, and executives—will have to develop the motivation and ability to portray Muslims and Muslim women objectively and realistically. The Institute for Social Policy and Understanding (ISPU), a nonprofit organization that conducts research and disseminates facts and research findings about Muslims to the public and policy makers, has written a guide for media professions: "Covering American Muslims Objectively and Creatively" (ISPU, 2021). This guide, which is available at ISPU"s website, provides facts about the Muslim community in the United States, and makes suggestions on how Muslims can be covered as a diverse group that is an important contributor to American society. Here is a summary of the guide (ISPU, 2021).

Myth Busters and Facts about Muslims

1. Large majorities of Muslims in the United States reject individual attacks against civilians (80%). Compared to Jews, Catholics, Protestants, White Evangelicals, and non-affiliated individuals, Muslims are more likely to reject military attacks on civilians (71%). The myth that Muslims are violent is not supported by these findings. According to the ISPU (2021), American Muslim leaders and organizations "have consistently and repeatedly denounced violent ideologies" (p. 9).
2. A total of 91% of Muslims with a strong religious identity also say they have strong American identities, compared to Muslims with weak

religious identity (68%). The majority of devout Muslims are not "extremists" who disavow being American; they also strongly identify as Americans, dispelling the myth that Muslims can't be Americans.

3. According to the FBI, White extremists and right-wing supremacists are responsible for far more violence and hate crimes in the United States than individuals who falsely claim that "Islam sanctions their crimes" (ISPU, 2021, p. 20).

4. Most American Muslim women choose how they dress: 99% say they wear hijab for personal reasons such as pity, to be identified as a Muslim, and modesty. This finding invalidates the myth that Muslim women do not have agency and are forced to wear hijab.

5. Muslim women are more educated and earn more than Muslim men; and represent a wide range of careers. Almost all consider Islam as a source of happiness and pride, and an important part of their identity. Therefore, the myth that Muslim women are submissive and without personal or religious agency is not supported by the data.

In addition to using these facts, ISPU (2021) suggests that media creators of news and entertainment should use accurate and unbiased language to portray Muslims objectively as Americans. Language to be avoided are:

1. Terrorist/terrorism to refer to ideological and non-ideological violence. Instead, use fact-based language to describe groups (militia, gunmen/women) and events, rather than using "terrorism" as a catch-all descriptor.

2. Islamist (ism). This term is often used to refer to "radical" extremism and terrorism when in fact, most Muslim reform movements (the traditional definition of Islamism) are nonviolent.

3. Sharia. When used out of context, "Sharia Law" is used in anti-Muslim propaganda to refer to alleged and perceived strict rules based on Islam that Muslim "extremists" wish to impose on non-Muslim Americans. In reality, Sharia means "Islam's recipe for a good life" (ISPU, 2021, p. 22) and has many interpretations accepted by Muslims, based on time and context.

4. "Unveil," in reference to Muslim women, suggests a lack of agency and that the veil represents their exploitation and oppression.

For objective and balanced portrayals, ISPU (2021) recommends that Muslims be presented in the diversity of everyday activities. Portrayals should not focus on acts of violence, repression of women, alleged acts of terrorism, national security issues, and to the binary between good Muslims who are opposed to extremism and bad Muslims (who commit acts of terror in the name of Islam). Another suggestion is for writers and reporters to avoid automatically assuming that religion (Islam) and ethnicity (Arab) are relevant to the story (ISPU, 2021).

Primes as Interventions

As the primary source of information about Muslims, television and newspaper news and entertainment can influence public perceptions and stereotypes of Muslims even with very brief reference. The mechanism by which this influence is accomplished is priming. As discussed in chapter 4, semantic and visual symbols can activate implicit stereotypes and affective perceptions of liking or disliking. Depending on the primes, these biases and applications can be positive or negative. Examples of negative primes are words referring to Muslims that the ISPU recommends not be used (e.g., terrorist, Islamist, jihad, unveiling). These words automatically invoke negative images and feelings toward Muslims. Positive primes are images and language about Muslim accomplishments in everyday life, contents that are not focused on violence, conflict, and the subjugation of women. These primes provide counter-stereotypes to prevailing negative narratives and symbols, a strategy shown by research to be highly effective in developing positive perceptions and neutralizing negative stereotypes and feelings. Examples of counter-stereotypes are a physician who is also a Muslim woman in a hijab; a decorated US military officer who is also a Muslim man or woman. The influence of primes in activating positive or negative bias cannot be understated, as decades of research have shown.

The effectiveness of balanced narratives and symbols—positive along with negative—in preventing the activation of negative stereotypes of Muslims is supported by activation control theories. Our proposition—tested in three studies discussed in chapter 6—is that strong negative primes can subconsciously provide the motivation for certain individuals to avoid using stereotypes in evaluating Muslims. The effectiveness of strong negative primes in activating stereotype control is supported in our Study 3 for Americans who identify as political liberals. Conservatives do not demonstrate the same result. In calling for balanced portrayals, the ISPU is not advocating for presentation of only positive portrays. Negative portrayals, when paired with positive portrayals may in fact perform a useful function in preventing the activation and use of negative stereotypes. Studies have shown that counter-stereotypes (positive portrayals) of a minority group are most effective in activating positive stereotypes when paired with negative stereotypes (negative portrayals) of the majority group (Dasgupta & Greenwald, 2001). Similarly, we expect balanced portrayals of Muslims to prevent the activation and use of negative stereotypes.

Chapter 8

Conclusions and Recommendations

When we started writing this book, our basic premises were first, that Muslim women were forgotten because of lack of attention from researchers and public policy makers, with most of the attention focused on Muslim men and threats they posed to American democracy; second, that public stereotypes and other perceptions of Muslim women were biased to reinforce prevailing stereotypes of Muslim men as terrorists and misogynists; third, that media portrayals of Muslim women reinforced biased public stereotypes; and fourth, that media portrayals included semantic and visual primes—shortcuts to more nuanced portrayals—that influenced public perceptions.

After primary and secondary research for the book, we have found support for these premises in varying degrees but more importantly, we have redirected some of our efforts toward identifying interventions that can mitigate the negative effects of prejudice directed at Muslim women. Among these interventions are media primes which can prevent the activation of stereotype use.

FORGOTTEN WOMEN?

A large body of research exists about Muslim women in Europe. Western European scholars for decades have studied how public stereotypes of Muslim women develop; narratives about Muslim women in newspapers, television, and social media and how these narratives influence public perceptions; how Muslim women cope with hate crimes and aggressive behaviors; how governments and private agencies are dealing with anti-Muslim hate crimes and aggressions. Some of the interesting findings are that spikes in hate crimes and other aggressions are linked to violent attacks against mainstream institutions and groups by people perceived to be "radical Muslims" and to stories in traditional media and chatter in social media about immigration. European studies also analyze links between bias toward Muslim women and anti-Muslim bias in general, racism, and other prejudices. Many studies are in-depth interviews with Muslim women to give them a voice and to bring to public attention aggressions against them.

In the United States, studies of Muslim women are only beginning to gain traction. For decades, researchers have studied public and media stereotypes of other American marginalized groups such as Blacks, Jews, and Hispanics. When Muslims are studied, the focus is on men and the "terrorist" dimension. Therefore, Muslim women are not "forgotten" in Europe but need more attention in the United States. This book is an attempt to draw more attention to Muslim women in the United States.

BIASED PUBLIC PERCEPTIONS

In doing our research, we were not surprised that national surveys by the Pew Research Organization and other agencies focused on Muslim men. When Muslim women are studied, the stereotype that emerges is that women are subservient to Muslim men. They do not have the freedom to act and dress as they want to; and they are accomplices to "terrorist" acts planned and implemented by Muslim men. We found that these misperceptions by the public are based on biased and incomplete information of Muslims in general but especially so for Muslim women. Large majorities of Americans admit that they know "very little" or "nothing" about Islam and that they do not know anyone who is a Muslim. Comparable data on lack of information is not available for Muslim women, but we would not be surprised if the ignorance is even higher. Compounding public images of Muslim women are the cultural frames in which they are judged. This is especially true for perceptions of hijab (religious attire) which are often based on American perceptions of appropriate social attire and gender norms in the United States.

MEDIA PORTRAYALS OF MUSLIM WOMEN

Since most Americans have little or no information about Muslims, major sources are the media and (mis)information in social media. A large majority of Americans say that they learn about Muslims from traditional and social media. When Muslims are covered in these media, themes of violence and refusal to integrate into American society predominate. When Muslim women are covered, even progressive newspapers like the *New York Times* and the *Washington Post* often focus on their lack of agency in restrictive Muslim societies, and "need to be liberated" themes. Therefore, information available to the American public about Muslims and Muslim women in particular are, with few exceptions, incomplete and biased toward American cultural norms and public policies (e.g., the "war on terror"). Our pre-book premise that American media coverage is biased is supported by our research, reinforcement of similar findings in Europe.

EFFECTS OF MEDIA COVERAGE AND PRIMES

Studies in Europe have established links between biased public perceptions and media use. The general finding is that the more media exposure particularly of perceived Muslim attacks and immigration, the more negative the perceptions of Muslims. Few studies in Europe and the United States have looked at Muslim women in particular but decades of research on media effects suggest that even brief exposure (as in laboratory experiments) to portrayals of a group can influence audience perceptions of the group. Put simply, positive portrayals lead to positive perceptions when there is a lack of previous information about the group, certainly true for Muslim women. Therefore, there is opportunity to identify through research which portrayals in particular (going past generalized "positive" and "negative") will neutralize negative stereotypes or lead to realistic, even positive, stereotypes, and to explain the processes that lead to the outcomes.

MEDIA PRIMES

Hijab is often identified as a visible marker of presumed identity of a woman as a Muslim. Some studies, including the three we completed for this book, have looked at how the hijab can prime negative perceptions and behavioral intentions. In the context of our studies, hijab is a prime that can activate implicit stereotypes and their application.

Primes, in general, have been found to be effective in stereotype activation. Skin tone, for example, influences the activation of stereotypes toward Blacks. Semantic primes affect perceptions of groups. Reference to Mexican immigrants as "thugs and rapists" lead to negative perceptions of Mexicans. Most people look for easy heuristics or strategies for making sense of a complex environment, such as other people who belong to out-groups. Rather than taking the time and effort to digest information, most people use semantic and visual primes that "stick out" and are repeated to form impressions or stereotypes of other people. Thus, primes are powerful agents of perception.

In three studies for this book, we found evidence of priming but with some unexpected results. The priming of negative stereotypes occurs for some people (e.g., self-identified conservatives). For liberals and college students, strong primes can have the opposite effect. Rather than priming negative stereotypes, strong primes can activate control of stereotype use so that evaluations become less negative. Therefore, a conclusion is that priming works differently based on education and political ideology. Our premise four—that media primes activate stereotypes—is supported but with the above caveat.

INTERVENTIONS, PRIMING, AND ACTIVATION CONTROL

For decades, research in social psychology and communication has identified interventions that can control or neutralize implicit biases and negative stereotyping of marginalized groups. Most of these studies have focused on implicit biases based on race, gender, age, and ethnicity. Few have considered biases toward Muslim women, although the interventions could also apply to Muslims in general and Muslim women in particular. Interventions that work generally begin with motivation to control biases; therefore, these interventions are proactive. The perceiver must initiate the process. However, motivations can be primed by signals and symbols such as those reminding the perceiver that equality is a basic value in American society, or by re-categorizing the target person (e.g., Muslim woman) so that latent stereotypes directed at one category (e.g., Muslim) are replaced by latent stereotypes directed at another group. Re-categorization can be primed by signs, words, and visuals, that portray counter-stereotypes of the targeted person.

A common counter-stereotype is a positive exemplar (positive examples) of the targeted person's group. Counter-stereotypes and exemplars contradict negative stereotypes associated with one category (e.g., Muslim). Studies of counter-stereotypes and exemplars show that they are most effective in neutralizing or replacing negative stereotypes when paired with negative exemplars of the mainstream group. For example, negative stereotypes are replaced with positive stereotypes when photos of admired Blacks are paired with photos of disliked Whites. Applied to Muslim women, balanced portrayals which include negative and positive portrayals can neutralize negative stereotypes. These portrayals could be summarized in words (e.g., "university professor" and "stay-at-home wife" in introducing a Muslim woman) or photos (a Muslim woman in a scientific laboratory and a Muslim woman in the

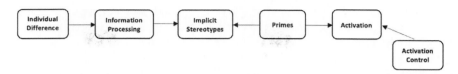

Figure 8.1   An Information-Processing Model of the Activation and Control of Implicit Stereotypes. *Source*: Created by authors.

ruins of a bombed building). These balanced primes motivate the perceiver to recalibrate his/her assessment of the target person, balancing negative and positive assessments. Activation control of stereotypes is facilitated among certain individuals (e.g., college students and liberals). The key strategy is to present balanced portrayals.

Theoretical Model

Figure 8.1 shows a theoretical model that maps out the processes and conditions of activation control of stereotypes from an information processing perspective.

In this model, individual differences such as education and political ideology influence how individuals process and respond to information including primes. A person's information-processing style in turn influences implicit stereotypes which can be activated by primes. Primes can also activate control of stereotypes and their application.

INDIVIDUAL DIFFERENCES, INFORMATION PROCESSING, AND STEREOTYPES

In this model, individual differences lead to distinctive information-processing styles. Individual differences often analyzed in studies of racism and ethnic bias are education, social conservatism, political ideology, gender, religion, political party affiliation, and age (Tan, 2021). Social conservatism, in particular, is related to racism and ethnic bias. Defined as "resistance to change and a desire to maintain existing social stratifications," social conservatism endorses socially conservative values such as law and order, punitive punishment for law breakers, social control, and adherence to traditional social conventions and traditions (Hodson & Busseri, 2012).

People who identify as social conservatives have a distinctive information processing style characterized as intolerance of ambiguity, a preference for simple answers, cognitive rigidity or a preference for "Yes" or "No" answers, cognitive inflexibility (less open to alternative perspectives), and less ability (compared to social liberals) to process and understand complex information (Jost et al., 2003; Sidanius, 1985; Stankov, 2009; Rokeach, 1984.) These markers of information processing have been observed in social conservatives even when education was controlled for (Hodson & Busseri, 2012).

In figure 8.1, information-processing style explained by individual differences influences stereotypes. Social conservatives, for example, are more likely than social liberals to be prejudiced, attributing negative stereotypes (consciously or unconsciously) to racial and ethnic minorities (e.g., Jost et al., 2003; Hodson & Busseri, 2012).

PRIMES, ACTIVATION, AND ACTIVATION CONTROL

Primes can activate unconscious stereotypes and their application. However, the influence of primes is moderated by social conservatism, conceptualized in our studies as ideological conservatism. Our studies show that primes activated negative stereotypes of Muslim women among political conservatives; the stronger the prime, the more negative the stereotypes and the more likely the negative stereotypes would be applied in evaluating Muslim women for a university teaching job. Among social liberals, stronger primes led to activation control of stereotypes and stereotype application, less negative stereotypes and less negative hiring evaluations. We conclude that self-identified liberals were more likely than conservatives to demonstrate activation control, particularly of behavioral intentions. While priming is more likely for affective evaluations such as stereotypes for both liberals and conservatives, activation control is more likely for stereotype application (such as behavioral intentions), particularly among liberals.

In sum, our model and studies recommend that research on priming should account for individual differences such as political and social ideology. The effects of priming on stereotypes and stereotype application depend on individual differences identified by research on prejudice and racism. By including these variables in the analysis, research can provide a clearer road map toward understanding when priming and activation control occur, and interventions that might work for targeted groups.

Bibliography

Abdeslam, A. A. (2020). Perceptions of Muslim women in French print media: Le Monde and Le Figaro as case studies. *Journal of Applied Language and Culture Studies pISSN, 2605*(3), 267–284.

Abele, A. E., Cuddy, A. J., Judd, C. M., & Yzerbyt, V. Y. (2008). Fundamental dimensions of social judgment. *European Journal of Social Psychology, 38*(7), 1063–1065.

Abraham, L. (1998). *Subtle manifestations of prejudice: Implicit visual constructions of black pathology.* Ph.D. Dissertation, Annenberg School for Communication, University of Pennsylvania.

Abraham, L. (2003). *Media stereotypes of African Americans. Images that injure: Pictorial stereotypes in the media* (2nd ed., pp. 87–92). Westport, CT: Praeger.

Abraham, L., & Appiah, O. (2006). Framing news stories: The role of visual imagery in priming racial stereotypes. *The Howard Journal of Communications, 17*(3), 183–203.

Abrajano, M., & Singh, S. (2009). Examining the link between issue attitudes and news source: The case of Latinos and immigration reform. *Political Behavior, 31*(1), 1–30.

Abu-Lughod, L. (2002). Do Muslim women really need saving? Anthropological reflections on cultural relativism and its others. *American Anthropologist, 3*, 783–790.

Abu-Lughod, L. (2013). *Do Muslim women need saving.* Harvard University Press.

Abu-Ras, W. M., & Suarez, Z. E. (2009). Muslim men and women's perception of discrimination, hate crimes, and PTSD symptoms post 9/11. *Traumatology, 15*(3), 48–63.

Agathangelou, A. M., & Ling, L. H. M. (2004). Power, borders, security, wealth: Lessons of violence and desire from September 11. *International Studies Quarterly, 48*, 517–538.

Ahmad, D. (2009). Not yet beyond the veil: Muslim women in American popular literature. *Social Text, 27*(2), 105–131.

Ahmed, L. (1992). *Women and gender in Islam: Historical roots of a modern debate.* New Haven: Yale University Press.

Ahmed, S., & Matthes, J. (2017). Media representation of Muslims and Islam from 2000 to 2015: A meta-analysis. *International Communication Gazette, 79*(3), 219–244.

Al-Saji, A. (2010). The racialization of Muslim veils: A philosophical analysis. *Philosophy & Social Criticism, 36*(8), 875–902.

Alimahomed-Wilson, S. (2017). Invisible violence: Gender, Islamophobia, and the hidden assault on U.S. Muslim women. *Women, Gender, and Families of Color, 5*(1), 73–97.

Allen, C. (2015). People hate you because of the way you dress: Understanding the invisible experience of veiled British Muslim women victims of Islamophobia. *International Journal of Victimology, 21*(3), 287–301.

Allport, G. W. (1954). *The nature of prejudice.* Addison-Wesley.

Alsultany, E. (2012). *Arabs and Muslims in the media.* New York University Press.

Altheide, D. (2000). Identity and the definition of the situation in a mass-mediated context. *Symbolic Interaction, 23*(1), 1–27.

Amir-Moazami, S. (2005). Muslim challenges to the secular consensus: A German case study. *Journal of Contemporary European Studies, 13*(3), 267–286.

Amz, T. (2014). Dismantling the stereotypes of Islam, Arab, and Muslim women in the visual and print media of the Western world. *Jurnal Kajian Komunikasi, 2*(2), 148–154.

Arendt, F. (2013). Dose dependent media priming effects of stereotypic newspaper articles on implicit and explicit stereotypes. *Journal of Communication, 63,* 830–851.

Aronson, E. (1988). *The social animal* (5th ed.). W.H. Freeman.

Arti, S. (2007). The evolution of Hollywood's representation of Arabs before 9/11: The relationship between political events and the notion of 'Otherness'. *Networking Knowledge: Journal of the MeCCSA Postgraduate Network, 1*(2), 1–20.

Asian American Journalists Association. (2020). Guide to covering Asian Pacific America. Asian American Journalists Association. Retrieved November 30, 2020, from https://www.aaja.org/2020/11/30/guide-to-covering-asian-pacific-america/ .

Aziz, S. (2012). From the oppressed to the terrorist: Muslim American women caught in the crosshairs of intersectionality. *Hastings Race & Poverty Law Journal, 9*(1), 191–264.

Badr, H. (2004). Islamic identity re-covered: Muslim women after September 11th. *Culture and Religion, 5*(3), 321–338.

Bahramitash, R. (2005). The war on terror, feminist orientalism and orientalist feminism: Case studies of two North American bestsellers. *Critique: Critical Middle Eastern Studies, 14*(2), 221–235.

Baker, P., Gabrielatos, C., & McEnery, T. (2013). *Discourse analysis and media attitudes: The representation of Islam in the British press.* Cambridge University Press.

Ball-Rokeach, S., Rokeach, M., & Grube, J. (1984). *The Great American values test.* The Free Press.

Bandura, A. (1986). *Social foundations of thought and action: A social cognitive theory.* Prentice-Hall.

Bandura, A. (2002). Social cognitive theory in cultural context. *Applied Psychology, 51*, 269–290.

Bargh, J., Schwader, K., Hailey, S., Dyer, R., & Boothby, E. (2012). Automaticity in social cognitive processes. *Trends in Cognitive Sciences, 16*(12), 593–605.

Barkdull, C., Khaja, K., Queiro-Tajalli, I., Swart, A., Cunningham, D., & Dennis, S. (2011). Experiences of Muslims in four Western countries post-9/11. *Affilia, 26*(2), 139–153.

Barker, C., & Galasinski, D. (2001). Language, culture, discourse. In *Cultural studies and discourse analysis: A dialogue on language and identity* (pp. 4–27). Sage.

Barreto, M. A., Manzano, S., & Segura, G. (2012). *The impact of media stereotypes on opinions and attitudes towards Latinos.* Pasadena, CA: National Hispanic Media Coalition and Latino Decisions.

Bartkoski, T., Lynch, E., Witt, C., & Rudolph, S. (2018). A meta-analysis of hiring discrimination against Muslims and Arabs. *Personnel Assessment and Decisions, 4*(2), 1–16.

Bartlett, T. (2005). The quiet heretic. *The Chronicle of Higher Education, 51*(49), A.10–A.12.

Baum, M. A. (2003). Soft news and political knowledge: Evidence of absence or absence of evidence? *Political Communication, 20*(2), 173–190.

Bayrakli, E., & Hafez, F. (2017). The state of Islamophobia in Europe. In E. Bayrakli & F. Hafez (Eds.), *European Islamophobia report 2016* (pp. 5–11). Ankara: SETA.

Behm-Morawitz, E., & Ortiz, M. (2013). Race, ethnicity, and the media. In Karen E. Dill (Ed.), *The Oxford handbook of media psychology* (pp. 252–266). Oxford: Oxford University Press.

Bertrand, M., & Mullainathan, S. (2004). Are Emily and Greg more employable than Lakisha and Jamal? A field experiment on labor market discrimination. *The American Economic Review, 94*(4), 991–1013.

Bhabha, H. K. (1994). *The location of culture.* Routledge.

Bhattacharyya, G. (2008). *Dangerous brown men: Exploiting sex, violence and feminism in the 'war on terror'.* Bloomsbury Publishing.

Bielen, S., Marneffe, W., & Mocan, N. (2018). Racial bias and in group bias in judicial decisions. Evidence from virtual reality courtrooms. NBER Working Paper No. w25355, Dec.

Blair, I. V. (2002). The malleability of automatic stereotypes and prejudice. *Personality and Social Psychology Review Social Psychology Review, 6,* 242–261.

Blair, I. V., & Banaji, M. (1996). Automatic and controlled processes in stereotype priming. *Journal of Personality and Social Psychology, 70*, 1142–1183.

Blair, I. V., Judd, L., & Chapleau, K. (2004). The influence of Afrocentric facial features in criminal sentencing. *Psychological Science, 15*(10), 674–679.

Blank, J. (1998). The Muslim mainstream. *U.S. News and World Report, 125*, 22–25.

Bleich, E., & Maurits van der V. (2020). *Covering Muslims: American newspapers in comparative perspective.* Unpublished manuscript.

Bowen, J. (2007). *Why the French don't like headscarves: Islam, the state, and public space.* Princeton, NJ: Princeton University Press.

Bowman, J. (2006).Warlord rules. *The New Criterion, 24*(7), 56–60.

Branton, R., & Dunaway, J. (2008). English- and Spanish- language media coverage of immigration: A comparative analysis. *Social Science Quarterly, 89*(4), 1006–1022.

Bridge Initiative Team. (2017). *A new era in American politics: The Trump administration and mainstream Islamophobia.* Georgetown University.

Brigham, J. C. (1971). Ethnic stereotypes. *Psychological Bulletin, 76*(1), 15.

Brown, C. S., Ali, H., Stone, E. A., & Jewell, J. A. (2017). US children's stereotypes and prejudicial attitudes toward Arab Muslims. *Analyses of Social Issues and Public Policy, 17*(1), 60–83.

Brown, M. D. (2006). Comparative analysis of mainstream discourses, media narratives and representations of Islam in Britain and France prior to 9/11. *Journal of Muslim Minority Affairs, 26*(3), 297–312.

Brummett, B. (2014). *Rhetoric in popular culture.* Thousand Oaks, CA: Sage.

Bullock, K., & Jafri, G. J. (2002). Media (Mis) representations: Muslim women in the Canadian nation. *Canadian Women's Studies, 20*(2), 35–40.

Byng, M. D. (2010). Symbolically Muslim: Media, hijab, and the West. *Critical Sociology, 36*(1), 109–129.

Cainkar, L. (2009). *Homeland insecurity: The Arab American and Muslim American experience after 9/11.* Russell Sage Foundation.

Calvo-Barbero, C., & Carrasco-Campos, Á. (2020). Portraits of Muslim women in the Spanish press: The" burkini" and" burqa" ban affair. *Communication & Society, 33*(1), 79–92.

Carpenter, F., Roskos-Ewoldson, D., & Roskos-Ewoldson, B. (2008). A test of the network models of political priming. *Media Psychology, 11*, 186–206.

Cesari, J. (2009). Citizenship: Western Europe – Brill. Retrieved June 8, 2020, from https://referenceworks.brillonline.com/entries/encyclopedia-of-women-and -islamic-cultures/citizenship-western-europe-EWICCOM_0068e

Chomsky, N. (1997). What makes mainstream media mainstream. *Zmagazine, 10*(10), 17–23.

Ciftci, S. (2012). Islamophobia and threat perceptions: Explaining anti-Muslim sentiment in the West. *Journal of Muslim Minority Affairs, 32*(3), 293–309.

Clifford, S., Jewell, R., & Waggoner, P. (2015). Are samples drawn from mechanical Turk valid for research on political ideology? *Research & Politics*, Oct-Dec., 1–9.

Cloud, D. L. (2004). "To veil the threat of terror": Afghan women and the⟨ clash of civilizations⟩ in the imagery of the US war on terrorism. *Quarterly Journal of Speech, 90*(3), 285–306.

Cohen, J. (1988). *Statistical power analysis for the behavioral sciences.* Lawrence Erlbaum Associates, Publishers.

Cook, D. (2005). Women fighting in Jihad? *Studies in Conflict and Terrorism, 28*, 375–384.

Cooke, M. (2002). Islamic feminism before and after September 11 (Afghan women's movement). *Duke Journal of Gender Law & Policy, 9*, 227.

Correll, J., Hudson, S. M., Guillermo, S., & Ma, D. S. (2014). The police officer's dilemma: A decade of research on racial bias in the decision to shoot. *Social and Personality Psychology Compass, 8*(5), 201–213.

Correll, J., Park, B., Judd, C. M., & Wittenbrink, B. (2002). The police officer's dilemma: Using ethnicity to disambiguate potentially threatening individuals. *Journal of Personality and Social Psychology, 83*, 1314–1329.

Correll, J., Park, B., Judd, C. M., & Wittenbrink, B. (2007). The influence of stereotypes on decisions to shoot. *European Journal of Social Psychology, 37*, 1102–1117.

Correll, J., Wittenbrink, B., Park, B., Judd, C. M., & Goyle, A. (2011). Dangerous enough: Moderating racial bias with contextual threat cues. *Journal of Experimental Social Psychology, 47*(1), 184–189.

Crenshaw, K. (1990). Mapping the margins: Intersectionality, identity politics, and violence against women of color. *Stanford Law Review, 43*, 1241.

Critelli, F. M. (2010). Beyond the veil in Pakistan. *Affilia, 25*, 236–249.

Cuddy, A. J., Fiske, S. T., & Glick, P. (2007). The BIAS map: Behaviors from intergroup affect and stereotypes. *Journal of Personality and Social Psychology, 92*(4), 631.

Dasgupta, N., & Greenwald, A. C. (2001). On the malleability of automatic attitudes: Combating automatic prejudice with images of admired and disliked individuals. *Journal of Personality and Social Psychology, 81*, 800–814.

DeAngelis, T. (2019). How does implicit bias by physicians affect patients' health care? *American Psychological Association, CE Corner, 50*(3), 22.

Devine, P. G. (1989). Stereotypes and prejudice: Their automatic and controlled components. *Journal of Personality and Social Psychology, 56*, 5–18.

Dioulgkaridou, E. (2021). The head-covering in Western Europe: Debates on Muslim women's integration in Germany and France.

Dixon, T. L. (2019). Media stereotypes: Content, effects, and theory. In *Media effects*. Taylor & Francis.

Dixon, T. L., & Williams, C. L. (2015). The changing misrepresentation of race and crime on network and cable news. *Journal of Communication, 65*(1), 24–39.

Donnell, A. (2003). Visibility, violence and voice? Attitudes to veiling post 11 September 2003. In *Veil: Veiling, representation and contemporary art* (pp. 122–135). MIT Press.

Dovidio, J. F., & Gaertner, S. L. (1986). *Prejudice, discrimination, and racism.* Academic Press.

Dwyer, C. (1999). Veiled meanings: Young British Muslim women and the negotiation of differences. *Gender, Place & Culture, 6*(1), 5–26.

Eberhardt, J., Goff, P., Purdie, V., & Davies, P. (2004). Seeing Black: Race, crime, and visual processing. *Journal of Personality and Social Psychology, 87*(6), 876–893.

el Feki, S. (2016). Women and Islam. In L. Pintak & S. Franklin (Eds.), *Islam for journalists (and Everyone Else)*. Retrieved from https://islamforjournalists.wordpress.com/

El Guindi, F. (1999). *Veil: Modesty, privacy and resistance.* iUniverse.

El Saadawi, N. (1980). *The hidden face of eve: Women in the Arab world* (Sherif Hetata, Trans.). London: Zed Books.

El-Aswad, E. S. (2013). Images of Muslims in Western scholarship and media after 9/11. *Digest of Middle East Studies, 22*(1), 39–56.

Eltantawy, N. M. A. (2007). *US newspaper representation of Muslim and Arab women post 9/11.* (Doctoral Dissertation). Georgia State University.

Entman R. M. (1993). Framing: Toward clarification of a fractured paradigm. *Journal of Communication, 43*, 51–58.

Entman, R. M. (1989). How the media affect what people think: An information processing approach. *The Journal of Politics, 51*(2), 347–370.

Entman, R. M. (1990). *Democracy without citizens: Media and the decay of American politics.* Oxford: Oxford University Press.

Esposito, J. L. (1999). *The Islamic threat: Myth or reality?* Oxford: Oxford University Press.

Essers, C., & Benschop, Y. (2009). Muslim businesswomen doing boundary work: The negotiation of Islam, gender and ethnicity within entrepreneurial contexts. *Human Relations, 62*(3), 403–423.

Everett, J. A., Schellhaas, F. M., Earp, B. D., Ando, V., Memarzia, J., Parise, C. V., ... & Hewstone, M. (2015). Covered in stigma? The impact of differing levels of I slamic head-covering on explicit and implicit biases toward M uslim women. *Journal of applied social psychology, 45*(2), 90–104.

Fahmy, S. (2004). Picturing Afghan women: A content analysis of AP wire photographs during the Taliban regime and after the fall of the Taliban regime. *Gazette (Leiden, Netherlands), 66*(2), 91–112.

Falah, G. W. (2005). I2 the visual representation of Muslim/Arab women in daily newspapers. In *Geographies of Muslim women: Gender, religion, and space* (p. 300). Guilford Press.

Farouqui, A. (2009). *Muslims and media images: News versus views.* New Delhi: Oxford University Press.

Fiske, S. T., Cuddy, A. J., Glick, P., & Xu, J. (2002). A model of (often mixed) stereotype content: Competence and warmth respectively follow from perceived status and competition. *Journal of Personality and Social Psychology, 82*(6), 878.

Fiske, S. T., Xu, J., Cuddy, A. C., & Glick, P. (1999). (Dis)respecting versus (dis) liking: Status and interdependence predict ambivalent stereotypes of competence and warmth. *Journal of Social Issues, 55*(3), 473–489.

Fiske, S. T. (1998). Stereotyping, prejudice and discrimination. In D. T. Gilbert, S. T. Fiske, & G. Lindzey (Eds.), *The handbook of social psychology* (pp. 357–411). McGraw-Hill.

FitzGerald, C., Martin, A., Berner, D., & Hurst, S. (2019). Interventions designed to reduce implicit prejudices and implicit stereotypes in real world contexts: A systematic review. *BMC Psychology, 7*(29). pp. 1–12.

Fleras, A., & Kunz, J. L. (2001). *Media and minorities: Representing diversity in a multicultural Canada.* Toronto: Thompson Educational Publishing, Inc.

Fowler, C. (2007). Journalists in feminist clothing: Men and women reporting Afghan women during Operation Enduring Freedom, 2001. *Journal of International Women's Studies, 8*(2), 4–19.

Gadarian, S. K. (2010). The politics of threat. *Journal of Politics, 72*(2), 469–483.

Gamson, W. A., Croteau, D., Hayes, W., & Sasson, T. (1992). Media images and the social construction of reality. *Annual Review of Sociology, 18*, 373–393.

García, A., Vives, A., Expósito, C., Pérez-Rincón, S., López, L., Torres, G., & Loscos, E. (2011). Velos, burkas, moros: estereotipos y exclusión de la comunidad musulmana desde una perspectiva de género. *Investigaciones feministas, 2*, 283–298.

Gardner, K. (2018). Social media: Where voices of hate find a place to preach. *Money and Democracy*, Aug. 30. https://hateinamerica.news21.com/

Gardner, R. C. (1973). Ethnic stereotypes: The traditional approach, a new look. *Canadian Psychologist/Psychologie canadienne, 14*(2), 133.

Gawronski, B., Greschke, D., & Banse, R. (2003). Implicit bias in impression formation: Associations influence the construal of individuating information. *European Journal of Social Psychology, 33*, 573–589.

GhaneaBassiri, K. (2013). Islamophobia and American history. In *Islamophobia in America* (pp. 53–74). Berlin: Springer.

Ghumman, S., & Ryan, R. (2013). Not welcome here: Discrimination towards women who wear the Muslim headscarf. *Human Relations, 66*(5), 671–698.

Gilbert, D. T., & Hixon, J. G. (1991). The trouble of thinking: Activation and application of stereotypic beliefs. *Journal of Personality and Social Psychology, 60*(4), 509–517.

Gilliam, F. D., Jr., & Iyengar, S. (2000). Prime suspects: The influence of local television news on the viewing public. *American Journal of Political Science, 44*(3), 560–573.

Gilliam, F. D., Jr., Iyengar S., Simon A., & Wright, O. (1996). Crime in Black and White. *Harvard International Journal of Press/Politics, 1*(3), 6–23.

Goldberg, D. T. (2006). Racial Europeanization. *Ethnic and Racial Studies, 29*(2), 331–364.

Gonsalkokorale, K., Sherman, J., & Klauer, K. (2009). Aging and prejudice: Diminished regulation of automatic race bias among older adults. *Journal of Experimental Social Psychology, 45*, 410–414.

Gottschalk, P., Greenberg, G., & Greenberg, G. (2008). *Islamophobia: Making Muslims the enemy*. Rowman & Littlefield.

Green, T. (2015). *The fear of Islam: An introduction to Islamophobia in the West.* Minneapolis: Fortress Press.

Greenwald, A. G., & Kriger, L. H. (2006). Implicit bias: Scientific foundations. *California Law Review, 94*(4), 945–967.

Greenwald, A. G., Poehlman, T., Uhlmann, E. L., & Banaji, N. R. (2009). Understanding and using the implicit association test: Meta-analysis of predictive validity. *Journal of Personality and Social Psychology, 97*, 17–41.

Greenwald, A. G., Smith, C. T., Siriam, N., Bar-Anan, Y., & Nosek, B. A. (2009). Race attitude measures predicted vote in the 2008 U.S. presidential election. *Analysis of Social Issues and Public Policy, 9*, 241–253.

Hall, S. (1990). The whites of their eyes: Racist ideologies and the media. In M. Alvarado & J. O. Thompson (Eds.), *The media reader* (pp. 7–23). London: BFI.

Hall, S. (1992). Cultural studies and its theoretical legacies. In L. Grossberg, C. Nelson & P. Treichler (Eds.), *Cultural studies* (pp. 277–294). New York: Routledge.

Hamilton, D. L., & Trolier, T. K. (1986). Stereotypes and stereotyping: An overview of the cognitive approach. In J. F. Dovidio & S. L. Gaertner (Eds.), *Prejudice, discrimination, and racism* (pp. 127–163). Academic Press.

Hauser, D. J., & Schwarz, N. (2016). Attentive Turkers: MTurk participants perform better on online attention checks than do subject pool participants. *Behavior Research Methods, 48*(1), 400–407.

Hennig, L. (2021). Islam at work: How Muslim women in France and Germany reconcile piety and profession. In *Exploring Islam beyond orientalism and occidentalism* (pp. 259–276). Wiesbaden: Springer VS.

Hilton, J. L., & Von Hippel, W. (1996). Stereotypes. *Annual Review of Psychology, 47*(1), 237–271.

Hirji, F. (2011). Through the looking glass: Muslim women on television-an analysis of 24, lost, and little mosque on the prairie. *Global Media Journal: Canadian Edition, 4*(2), 33–47

Hirschkind, C., & Mahmood, S. (2002). Feminism, the Taliban, and politics of counterinsurgency. *Anthropological Quarterly, 75*(2), 339–354.

Hodson, G., & Busseri, M. (2012). Bright minds and dark attitudes: Lower cognitive ability predicts greater prejudice through right-wing ideology and low intergroup contact. *Psychological Science, 23*(2), 187–195.

Human Rights Council. (2021). Countering Islamophobia/anti-Muslim hatred to eliminate discrimination and intolerance based on religion or belief. Report of the Special Rapporteur on freedom of religion or belief.

Ibroscheva, E., & Ramaprasad, J. (2008). Do media matter? A social construction model of stereotypes of foreigners. *Journal of Intercultural Communication, 16.* Retrieved from: https://www.immi.se/intercultural/nr16/ibroscheva.htm

Institute for Social Policy and Understanding. (2021). *Covering Muslims objectively and creatively: A guide for media professionals.* Retrieved from: https://www.ispu.org/wp-content/uploads/2020/04/ISPU_MediaGuide_digital.pdf?x46312

Issaka, B. (2021). *Alienating: How the portrayal of Muslim women in US media affects Muslim women's social identities* (Master's Thesis). Kansas State University.

Iyengar, S., Kinder, D., Peters, M., & Krosnick, J. (1984). The evening news and presidential evaluations. *Journal of Personality and Social Psychology, 46*, 778–787.

Iyengar, S., Peters M. D., & Kinder, D. R. (1982). Experimental demonstrations of the 'not-so-minimal' consequences of television news programs. *American Political Science Review, 76*(4), 848–858.

Jackson, L. (2010). Images of Islam in US Media and their Educational Implications, *Educational Studies, 46*(1), 3–24, DOI: 10.1080/00131940903480217

Janson, E. (2011). Stereotypes that define 'us': The case of Muslim women. *ENDC Proceedings, 14*, 181–196.

Jawad, H., & Benn, T. (2002). *Muslim women in the United Kingdom and beyond: Experiences and images.* Brill.

Jiwani, Y. (2005). "War Talk" engendering terror: Race, gender and representation in Canadian print media. *International Journal of Media and Cultural Politics, 1*(1), 15–22.

Johnson, K. (2019). The priming of Arab-Israeli stereotypes: How news stories may enhance or inhibit audience stereotypes. *Journal of International Women's Studies, 20*(21), 225–240.

Jones, J. M. (1997). *Prejudice and racism.* McGraw-Hill Humanities, Social Sciences & World Languages.

Joseph, S., D'Harlingue, B., & Wong, A. (2008). Arab Americans and Muslim Americans in the New York Times, before and after 9/11. In A. A. Jamal & N. C. Naber (Eds.), *Race and Arab Americans before and after 9/11: From invisible citizens to visible subjects* (pp. 229–275). Syracuse: Syracuse University Press.

Jost, J. T., Glaser, J., Kruglanski, A. W., & Sulloway, F. J. (2003). Political conservatism as motivated social cognition. *Psychological Bulletin, 129*(3), 339–375.

Kabir, N. (2004). *Muslims in Australia: Immigration, Race Relations and Cultural History* (pp. 272–284). London: Kegan Paul.

Kahf, M. (2011). The Pity Committee and the careful reader: How not to buy stereotypes about Muslim women. In *Arab and Arab American feminisms: Gender, violence, and belonging.* Syracuse, New York: Syracuse University Press.

Kalkan, K. O., Layman, G. C., & Uslaner, E. M. (2009). "Bands of others"? Attitudes toward Muslims in contemporary American society. *The Journal of Politics, 71*(3), 847–862.

Kassam, A. (2008). The weak, the powerless, the oppressed: Muslim women in Toronto media. *Canadian Journal of Media Studies, 4*(1), 71–88.

Katz, D., & Braly, K. (1933). Racial stereotypes of one hundred college students. *The Journal of Abnormal and Social Psychology, 28*(3), 280.

Katz, P. A. (2003). Racists or tolerant multiculturalists: How do they begin? *American Psychologist, 58*(11), 897–909.

Kaya, I. (2007). Muslim American identities and diversity. *Journal of Geography, 106*(1), 29–35.

Kearns, E. M., Betus, A. E., & Lemieux, A. F. (2019). Why do some terrorist attacks receive more media attention than others?. *Justice Quarterly, 36*(6), 985–1022.

Keller, S. W. (2010). Abstract reasoning as a predictor of attitudes toward gay men. *Journal of Homosexuality, 57*, 914–927.

Kellner, D. (2004). 9/11, spectacles of terror, and media manipulation: A critique of Jihadist and Bush media politics. *Critical Discourse Studies, 1*(1), 41–64.

Kellstedt, P. M. (2003). *The mass media and the dynamics of American racial attitudes.* Cambridge: Cambridge University Press.

Kellstedt, P. M. (2005). Media frames, core values, and the dynamics of racial policy preferences. In K. Callaghan & F. Schnell (Eds.), *Framing American politics* (pp. 167–178). Pittsburgh: University of Pittsburgh Press.

Kervyn, N., Fiske, S. T., & Yzerbyt, V. Y. (2013). Integrating the stereotype content model (warmth and competence) and the Osgood semantic differential (evaluation, potency, and activity). *European Journal of Social Psychology, 43*(7), 673–681.

Kidder, C., White, K., Hinojos, M., Sandoval, M., & Crites Jr., L. (2018). Sequential stereotype priming: A meta-analysis. *Personality and Social Psychology Review, 22*, 199–227.

Klaus, E., & Kassel, S. (2005). The veil as a means of legitimization: An analysis of the interconnectedness of gender, media and war. *Journalism, 6*(3), 335–355.

Knowles, E., Lowery, B., & Schaumberg, R. (2010). Racial prejudice predicts opposition to Obama and his health care reform plan. *Journal of Experimental Social Psychology, 46*(2), 420–423.

Kumar, D. (2010). Framing Islam: The resurgence of Orientalism during the Bush II era. *Journal of Communication Inquiry, 34*(3), 254–277.

Kwan, M.-P. (2008). From oral histories to visual narratives: Re-presenting the post-September 11 experiences of the Muslim Women in the USA. *Social and Cultural Geography, 9*, 653–669.

La Ferle, C., & Lee, W. N. (2005). Can English language media connect with ethnic audiences? Ethnic minorities' media use and representation perceptions. *Journal of Advertising Research, 45*(1), 140–153.

Lajevardi, N. (2021). The media matters: Muslim American portrayals and the effects on mass attitudes. *The Journal of Politics, 83*(3), 1060–1079.

Lamrabet, A. (2014). El velo (el hiyab) de las mujeres musulmanas: entre la ideología colonialista y el discurso islámico: una visión decolonial. *Tabula Rasa, 21*, 31–46.

Lang, A. (2000). The limited capacity model of mediated message processing. *Journal of Communication, 50*, 46–70.

Laster, K., & Erez, E. (2015). Sisters in terrorism? Exploding stereotypes. *Women & Criminal Justice, 25*(1–2), 83–99.

Levinson, J. D., & Young, D. (2010). Different shades of bias: Skin tone, implicit racial bias, and judgments of ambiguous evidence. *West Virginia Law Review, 112*, 307–339.

Ling, L. H. M. (1999). Sex machine: Global hypermasculinity and images of the Asian woman in modernity. *Positions: East Asia Cultures Critique, 7*(2), 277–306.

Livingston, R. W., & Brewer, M. B. (2002). What are we really priming? Cue-based versus category-based processing of facial stimuli. *Journal of Personality and Social Psychology, 82*(1), 5–18.

Luttig, M. D., Federico, C. M., & Lavine, H. (2017). Supporters and opponents of Donald Trump respond differently to racial slurs: An experimental analysis. *Research and Politics, 4*(4), 1–8.

Lyons, I. (2009). *Public perceptions of older people and aging.* National Center for the Protection of Older People.

Macdonald, M. (2006). Muslim women and the veil: Problems of image and voice in media representations. *Feminist Media Studies, 6*(1), 7–23.

Macrae, C. N., Bodenhausen, G. V., & Milne, A. B. (1995). The dissection of selection in person perception. Inhibitory processes in social stereotyping. *Journal of Personality and Social Psychology, 69*, 397–407.

Mahmood, S. (2009). Feminism, democracy, and empire: Islam and the war on terror. In *Gendering religion and politics* (pp. 193–215). New York: Palgrave Macmillan.

Mahmood, S. (2011). *Politics of piety.* Princeton University Press.

Mahmoud, S. (2002). Feminism, the Taliban, and politics of counterinsurgency. *Anthropological Quarterly, 2*, 339–354.

Maira, S. (2009). "Good" and "bad" Muslim citizens: Feminists, terrorists, and US orientalisms. *Feminist Studies, 35*(3), 631–656.

Maira, S. (2011). Islamophobia and the war on terror: Youth, citizenship and dissent. In J. L. Esposito & I. Kalin (Eds.), *Islamophobia: The challenge of pluralism in the 21st century* (pp. 119–125). New York: Oxford University Press.

Martin, P., & Phelan, S. (2002). Representing Islam in the wake of September 11: A comparison of US television and CNN online message board discourses. *Prometheus, 20*(3), 263–269.

Mastro, D. (2009). Effects of racial and ethnic stereotyping. In J. Bryant & M. B. Oliver (Eds.), *Media effects: Advances in theory and research* (pp. 325–341). Taylor and Francis.

McCombs, M., & Valenzuela, S. (2020). *Setting the agenda: Mass media and public opinion.* John Wiley & Sons.

McConnell, A., & Leibold, J. (2001). Relations among the Implicit Association Test, discriminatory behavior, and explicit measures of racial attitudes. *Journal of Experimental and Social Psychology, 37*(5), 435–442.

Medina, J. (2008). *Brain rules: 12 principles for surviving and thriving at work, home and school.* Seattle, WA: Pear Press.

Merolla, J., & Zechmeister, E. J. (2009). *Democracy at risk: How terrorist threats affect the public.* Chicago: University of Chicago Press.

Mescoli, E. (2016). *Forgotten women: The impact of Islamophobia on Muslim women.* Brussels: European Network Against Racism (ENAR).

Milinković, A. (2014). *Muslim women in the media after 9/11. A content analysis of the American and British digital media between 2001 and 2002* (Bachelor's Thesis). University of Iceland.

Mishra, S. (2007). Saving Muslim women and fighting Muslim men: Analysis of representations in the New York Times. *Global Media Journal, 6*(11), 1–20.

Moaddel, M. (2002). The study of Islamic culture and politics: An overview and assessment. *Annual Review of Sociology, 28*(1), 359–386.

Mondon, A., & Winter, A. (2017). Articulations of Islamophobia: From the extreme to the mainstream? *Ethnic and Racial Studies, 40*(13), 2151–2179.

Monteith, M. J., & Spicer, C. V. (2000). Contents and correlates of Whites' and Blacks' racial attitudes. *Journal of Experimental Social Psychology, 36*(2), 125–154.

Moors, A., & Tarlo, E. (2013). Fashion and its discontents: The aesthetics of covering in the Netherlands. *Islamic fashion and anti-fashion: New perspectives from Europe and North America.* London, UK: Bloomsbury Academic (p. 241).

Moskowitz, G. B., & Stone, J. (2012). The proactive control of stereotype activation: Implicit goals to not stereotype. *Zeitschrift for Psychologie, 220*, 172–179.

Moss-Racusin, C. A., Dovidio, J. F., Brescoll, V. L., Graham, M., & Handelsman, J. (2012). Science faculty's subtle gender biases favor male students. *Proceedings of the National Academy of Science, 109*(41), 16474–16479.

Muller, F., & Rothermund, K. (2014). What does it take to activate stereotypes? Simple primes don't seem enough: a replication of stereotype activation. *Social Psychology, 45*, 187–193.

Murphy, N. A., & Hall, J. A. (2011). Intelligence and interpersonal sensitivity: A meta-analysis. *Intelligence, 39*, 54–63.

Muscati, S. A. (2002). Arab/Muslim 'otherness': The role of racial constructions in the Gulf War and the continuing crisis with Iraq. *Journal of Muslim Minority Affairs, 22*(1), 131–148.

Nacos, B. L., Nacos, B., & Torres-Reyna, O. (2007). *Fueling our fears: Stereotyping, media coverage, and public opinion of Muslim Americans.* Rowman & Littlefield.

Nacos, B. L., & Torres-Reyna, O. (2002). *Muslim Americans in the news before and after 9-11.* Paper presented at the Restless Searchlight: Terrorism, the Media and Public Life Symposium, Cambridge, MA.

Naficy, H. (2003). Poetics and politics of veil, voice, and vision in Iranian postrevolutionary cinema: Veiling, representation and contemporary art. In *Veil: Veiling, representation and contemporary art* (pp. 136–159). The MIT Press.

Nayak, M. (2006). Orientalism and 'saving' US state identity after 9/11. *International Feminist Journal of Politics, 8*(1), 42–61.

Nisbet, E. C., Ostman, R., & Shanahan, J. (2008). Public opinion toward Muslim Americans: Civil liberties and the role of religiosity, ideology, and media use. In A. Sinno (Ed.), *Muslims in Western politics* (pp. 161–199). Bloomington: Indiana University Press.

Nosek, B. A., Greenwald, A. G., & Banaji, M. R. (2007). The Implicit Association Test at age 7: A methodological and conceptual review. In J. A. Bargh (Ed.), *Automatic processes in social thinking and behavior* (pp. 265–292). Psychology Press.

Nosek, B. A., Hawkins, C., & Frazier, R. (2011). Implicit social cognition: From measures to mechanisms. *Trends in Cognitive Sciences, 15*(4), 152–159.

Oliver, M. B., & Fonash, D. (2002). Race and crime in the news: Whites' identification and misidentification of violent and nonviolent criminal suspects. *Media Psychology, 4*(2), 137–156.

Orbe, M. P., & Harris, T. M. (2013). *Interracial communication: Theory into practice.* SAGE Publications.

Organization for Security and Co-operation in Europe. (2013). *Women and terrorist radicalization: Final report.* Vienna, Austria: OSCE-ODIHR. Retrieved from http://www.osce.org/secretariat/99919

Osgood, C. E., Suci, G. J., & Tannenbaum, P. H. (1957). *The measurement of meaning* (No. 47). University of Illinois Press.

Panagopoulos, C. (2006). The polls-trends: Arab and Muslim Americans and Islam in the aftermath of 9/11. *International Journal of Public Opinion Quarterly, 70*(4), 608–624.

Perry, B. (2014). Gendered Islamophobia: Hate crime against Muslim women. *Social Identities, 20*(1), 74–89.

Pettigrew, T. F. (2017). Social psychological perspectives on Trump supporters. *Journal of Social and Political Psychology, 5*(10), 107–116.

Pew Research Center. (2009). *Muslims widely seen as facing discrimination: Views of religious similarities and differences.* Retrieved from https://www.pewresearch.org/politics/2009/09/09/muslims-widely-seen-as-facing-discrimination/

Pew Research Center. (2014). *How Americans feel about religious groups.* Pew Research Center. Retrieved from http://www.pewforum.org/2014/07/16/how-americans-feel-about-religious-groups/

Pew Research Center. (2017). *Muslims and Islam: Key findings in the U.S. and around the world.* Retrieved from https://www.pewresearch.org/fact-tank/2017/08/09/muslims-and-islam-key-findings-in-the-u-s-and-around-the-world/

Pew Research Center. (2020). Women in many countries face harassment for clothing deemed too religious – or too secular. Retrieved from https://www.pewresearch.org/fact-tank/2020/12/16/women-in-many-countries-face-harassment-for-clothing-deemed-too-religious-or-too-secular/

Pintak, L., Bowe, B. J., & Albright, J. (2019, March 13). Islamophobes came for Americans on the Campaign Trail. *Foreign Policy.* https://foreignpolicy.com/2019/03/13/islamophobes-came-for-americans-on-the-campaign-trail/

Pittman, C. (2020). Shopping while Black: Black consumers' management of racial stigma and racial profiling in retail settings. *Journal of Consumer Culture, 20*(1), 3–22.

Posetti, J. (2007). Unveiling news coverage of Muslim women: Reporting in the age of terror. *International Journal of Diversity in Organizations, Communities and Nations, 7*(5), 69–79.

Powell, K. A. (2011). Framing Islam: An analysis of US media coverage of terrorism since 9/11. *Communication Studies, 62*(1), 90–112.

Predelli, L. N. (2004). Interpreting gender in Islam: A case study of immigrant Muslim women in Oslo, Norway. *Gender & Society, 18*(4), 473–493.

Prior, M. (2005). News vs. entertainment: How increasing media choice widens gaps in political knowledge and turnout. *American Journal of Political Science, 49*(3), 577–592.

Puar, J. K. (2007). Introduction: Homonationalism and biopolitics. In *Terrorist Assemblages* (pp. 1–36). Duke University Press.

Rachilinski, J., Johnson, S. L., Wistrich, A. J., & Guthrie, C. (2009). Does unconscious racial bias affect trial judges? *Notre Dame Law Review, 84*(3), 1195–1246.

Rahman, K. A. (2020). News media and the Muslim identity after the Christchurch mosque massacres. *Kōtuitui: New Zealand Journal of Social Sciences Online, 15*(2), 360–384.

Rahmath, S., Chambers, L., & Wakewich, P. (2016). Asserting citizenship: Muslim women's experiences with the hijab in Canada. *Women's Studies International Forum, 58*, 34–40.

Ramasubramanian, S. (2007). Media-based strategies to reduce racial stereotypes activated by news stories. *Journalism and Mass Communication Quarterly, 84*, 249–264.

Rao, K., & Shenkman, C. (2018). *Equal treatment? Measuring the media and legal responses to ideologically motivated violence in the United States.* Institute for Social Policy and Understanding.

Razack, S. (2008). *Casting out: The eviction of Muslims from Western law and politics.* University of Toronto Press.

Richardson, J. E. (2004). *(Mis)representing Islam: The racism and rhetoric of British broadsheet newspapers.* Philadelphia, PA: John Benjamins.

Rokeach, S., Rokeach, M., & Grube, J. (1984). *The great American values test: Influencing behavior and beliefs thru television.* Free Press.

Rooth, D. (2010). Automatic associations and discrimination to hiring: Real world evidence. *Labour Economics, 17*, 523–534.

Roskos-Ewoldson, D. R., Klinger, M. R., & Roskos-Ewoldson, B. R. (2007). Media priming: A meta analysis. In R. W. Preiss, B. M. Gayle, N. Burrell, M. Allen, & J. Bryant (Eds.), *Mass media effects research* (pp. 53–80). Mahwah, NJ: Erlbaum.

Rudman, L., Ashmore, R., & Gary, M. (2001). "Unlearning" automatic biases: The malleability of implicit prejudice and stereotypes. *Journal of Personality and Social Psychology, 81*(5), 856–868.

Rudman, L. A. (2004). Sources of implicit attitudes. *Current Directions in Psychological Science, 13*, 80–83.

Runnymede Trust. (2017). *Islamophobia still a challenge for us all.* London: Runnymede Trust.

Saeed, A. (2007). Media, racism and Islamophobia: The representation of Islam and Muslims in the media. *Sociology Compass, 1*(2), 443–462.

Saha, A. (2012). Beards, scarves, halal meat, terrorists, forced marriage: Television industries and the production of race. *Media, Culture and Society, 34*(4), 424–438.

Said, E. W. (1978). *Orientalism: Western conceptions of the Orient.* London: Pantheon Books.

Said, E. (1979). *Orientalism.* New York: Vintage.

Saleem, M., Prot, S., Anderson, C. A., & Lemieux, A. F. (2017). Exposure to Muslims in media and support for public policies harming Muslims. *Communication Research, 44*(6), 841–869.

Schaffner, B. F. (2018). Follow the racist: The consequences of Trump's expression of prejudice for mass rhetoric. *Semantic Scholar.*

Schneider, D. J. (2004). *The psychology of stereotyping.* New York, NY: The Guilford Press.

Secor, A. (2002). The veil and urban space in Istanbul: Women's dress, mobility and Islamic knowledge. *Gender, Place and Culture, 9*(1), 5–22.

Selod, S., & Embrick, D. G. (2013). Racialization and Muslims: Situating the Muslim experience in race scholarship. *Sociology Compass, 7*(8), 644–655.

Selod, S. (2015). Citizenship denied: The racialization of Muslim American men and women post-9/11. *Critical Sociology, 41*(1), 77–95.

Seta, D. (2016). *Forgotten women: The impact of Islamophobia on Muslim women.* European Network against Racism.

Shaheen, J. (2008). *Guilty, Hollywood's verdict on Arabs after 9/11.* Olive Branch Press.

Shaheen, J. G. (2003). Reel bad Arabs: How Hollywood vilifies a people. *The ANNALS of the American Academy of Political and Social Science, 588*(1), 171–193.

Sheen, M., Yekani, H., & Jordan, T. (2018). Investigating the effect of wearing the hijab: Perception of facial attractiveness by Emirati Muslim women living in their native Muslim country. *Journal of Applied Social Psychology, 45*, 90–104.

Shepherd, L. J. (2006). Veiled references: Constructions of gender in the Bush administration discourse on the attacks on Afghanistan post-9/11. *International Feminist Journal of Politics, 8*(1), 19–41.

Sheridan, L. P. (2006). Islamophobia pre–and post–September 11th, 2001. *Journal of Interpersonal Violence, 21*(3), 317–336.

SibAi, S. A. (2014). El «hiyab» en la obra de Fátima Mernissi o la paradoja del silenciamiento. Hacia un pensamiento islámico decolonial. *Tabula Rasa, 21*, 47–76.

Sidanius, J. (1985). Cognitive functioning and sociopolitical ideology revisited. *Political Psychology, 6*(4), 637–661.

Sides, J., & Gross, K. (2013). Stereotypes of Muslims and support for the war on terror. *The Journal of Politics, 75*(3), 583–598.

Signorielli, N., Morgan, M., & Shanahan, J. (2019). The violence profile: Five decades of cultural indicators research. *Mass Communication and Society, 22*, 1–28.

Soltani, A. (2016). Confronting prejudice against Muslim women in the West, United Nations University. Retrieved from https://unu.edu/publications/articles/confronting-prejudice-against-muslim-women-in-the-west.html.

Spivak, G. C. (1994). Can the subaltern speak? In P. Williams & L. Chrisman (Eds.), *Colonial discourse and post-colonial theory: A reader* (pp. 93). Hertfordshire: Harvester Wheatsheaf.

Stankov, I. (2009). Conservatism and cognitive ability. *Intelligence, 37*(3), 294–304.

Starr, S. (2016). Testing racial profiling: Empirical assessment of disparate treatment by police. *University of Chicago Legal Forum*, 485–531.

Steet, L. (2000). *Veils and daggers: A century of national geographic's representation of the Arab World.* Philadelphia: Temple University Press.

Steinberg, S. R. (2002). French fries, fezzes, and minstrels: The Hollywoodization of Islam. Cultural Studies? *Critical Methodologies*, 2(2), 205–210.

Stephan, W. G., Ageyev, V., Stephan, C. W., Abalakina, M., Stefanenko, T., & Coates-Shrider, L. (1993). Measuring stereotypes: A comparison of methods using Russian and American samples. *Social Psychology Quarterly*, 56(1), 54–64.

Stephan, W. G., & Stephan, C. W. (2000). An integrated theory of prejudice. In S. Oskamp (Ed.), *Reducing prejudice and discrimination* (pp. 21–46). Lawrence Erlbaum and Associates Publishers.

Strabac, Z., & Valenta, M. (2012). Attitudes toward Muslims in Norway. In M. Helbling (Eds.), *Islamophobia in Western Europe and North America: Measuring and explaining individual attitudes (Routledge advances in sociology)* (pp. 57–69). Hoboken: Taylor & Francis.

Swisher, S. B. (2019). *Gendered Islamophobia and sense of belonging: Experiences of visibly Muslim women in higher education* (Doctoral dissertation, Fordham University).

Tajfel, H. (1979). Individuals and groups in social psychology. *British Journal of Clinical and Social Psychology, 18*(2), 183–190.

Tan, A. (2021). *Communication and prejudice: Theories, effects and interventions* (third ed.). Cognella Academic Publishing.

Tan, A., Fujioka, Y., & Tan, G. (2000). Television use, stereotypes of African Americans and opinions on affirmative action: An affective model of policy reasoning. *Communications Monographs, 67*(4), 362–371.

Tan, A., Vishnevskaya, A., & Khan, H. (2019). *Semantic and visual primes of stereotypes of Muslim women: Evaluative and behavioral consequences.* Toronto, Canada: AEJMC.

Terman, R. (2017). Islamophobia and media portrayals of Muslim women: A compu-
tational text analysis of US news coverage. *International Studies Quarterly, 61*(3),
489–502.

Traugott, M., Brader, T., Coral, D., Curtin, R., Featherman, D., Groves, R., ... Willis,
R. (2002). How Americans responded: A study of public reactions to 9/11/01. *PS:
Political Science & Politics, 35*(3), 511–516.

Trevino, M., Kanso, A. M., & Nelson, R. A. (2010). Islam through editorial lenses:
How American elite newspapers portrayed Muslims before and after September 11,
2001. *Journal of Arab and Muslim Media Research, 3*(1–2), 3–17.

Unkelbach, C., Forgas, J. P., & Denson, T. F. (2008). The turban effect: The influence
of Muslim headgear and induced affect on aggressive responses in the shooter bias
paradigm. *Journal of Experimental Social Psychology, 44*(5), 1409–1413.

Valdés-Peña, A. (2013). La creación de la identidad de la mujer musulmana en
la prensa desde la Teoría del Enfoque. In M. Fernández-Montes (Coord.),
Negociaciones identitarias en contextos migratorios (pp. 235–246). Madrid:
Common Ground Publishing.

Van Dijk, T. (1991). *Racism and the press*. London: Routledge.

Van Dijk, T. A. (1995). Power and the news media. *Political Communication and
Action, 6*(1), 9–36.

Van Es, M. A. (2019). Muslim women as 'ambassadors' of Islam: Breaking
stereotypes in everyday life. *Identities, 26*(4), 375–392.

Varisco, D. M. (2005). *Islam obscured: The rhetoric of anthropological representation*.
New York: Palgrave Macmillan.

Verhaeghen, P., Aikman, S., & Van Gulick, A. (2011). Prime and prejudice:
Co-occurrence in the culture as a source of automatic stereotype priming. *British
Journal of Social Psychology, 50*(3), 501–518.

Viorst, M. (1994). *Sandcastles: The Arabs in search of the modern world*. New York:
Alfred A. Knopf.

Vishnevskaya, A., Khan, H., & Tan, A. (2020). *Semantic and visual primes of Muslim
women: Evaluative and behavioral consequences*. San Francisco, CA: AEJMC.

Wagner, W., Sen, R., Permanadeli, R., & Howarth, C. S. (2012). The veil and Muslim
women's identity: Cultural pressures and resistance to stereotyping. *Culture &
Psychology, 18*(4), 521–541.

Walters, S., & Mouhktar, S. (2019). 'I love the freedoms here, but I still miss home.'
Muslim women's perceptions of how social contact optimized wellbeing and personal commitments to faith. *Journal of Muslim Mental Health, 13*(2), 45–83.

Ward, L. (2001). Leaders' wives join propaganda war. Retrieved from https://www
.theguardian.com/uk/2001/nov/17/afghanistan.september11.

Wasserstein, R. L., Schirm, A. L., & Lazar, N. A. (2019). Moving to a world beyond
"p<0.05". *The American Statistician, 73*, 1–19.

Watson, H. (1994). Women and the veil. In *Islam, globalization and postmodernity*
(pp. 141–159). London: Routledge.

Watt, D. P. (2012). The urgency of visual media literacy in our post-9/11 world:
Reading images of Muslim women in the print news media. *Journal of Media
Literacy Education, 4*(1), 32–43.

Weston, M. A. (2003). Post 9/11 Arab American coverage avoids stereotypes. *Newspaper Research Journal, 24*(1), 92–106.

Wilkins, K. G. (1995). Middle Eastern women in Western eyes. In *The US media and the Middle East: Image and perception* (pp. 50–61). Santa Barbara, CA: Greenwood.

Wortley, S., Hagan J., & Macmillan, R. (1997). Just Des(s)erts? The racial polarization of perceptions of criminal injustice. *Law and Society Review, 31*(4), 637–676.

Yazbeck Haddad, Y. (2007). The post-9/11 Hijab as icon. *Sociology of Religion, 68*(3), 253–267.

Zahedi, A. (2011). Muslim American women in the post-11 September era: Challenges and opportunities. *International Feminist Journal of Politics, 13*(2), 183–203.

Zempi, I. (2016). Negotiating constructions of insider and outsider status in research with veiled Muslim victims of Islamophobic hate crime. *Sociological Research, 21*(4), 70–81.

Ziegert, J. C., & Hanges, P. J. (2005). Employment discrimination: The role of implicit attitudes, motivation, and a climate for racial bias. *Journal of Applied Social Psychology, 90*(3), 553–562.

Zine, J. (2006). Between orientalism and fundamentalism: The politics of Muslim women's feminist engagement. *Muslim World Journal of Human Rights, 3*(1), 1–24.

Index

About the Authors

Alexis Tan has a PhD in mass communication from the University of Wisconsin-Madison. He is a professor of communication and was the inaugural University Faculty Diversity Fellow and the founding director of the Edward R. Murrow School of Communication (1990–2006) at Washington State University. The recipient of a Senior Fulbright Award, he has lectured and done research in over 20 countries. He has written over 60 journal articles and book chapters and is the author of several books: *Mass Communication Theories and Research* (first and second editions); *The Intercultural Communication Guidebook: Research-based Strategies for Successful Interactions*; *Communication and Prejudice: Theories, Effects, and Interventions* (first, second, and third editions), *Global Communication and Media Research* (2018), and *Who is Racist? Why Racism Matters* (2020). He is a past president of the Association for Education in Journalism and Mass Communication.

Anastasia Vishnevskaya is a PhD candidate in the Edward R. Murrow College of Communication at Washington State University, with expected graduation in May 2023. Using quantitative and qualitative methods, she studies and writes on the effects that stereotypes and image politics have on public opinion as well as on effective interventions to mitigate the negative effects of bias. In addition to this book, she has published and presented conference papers in collaboration with faculty and other graduate students. Her recent collaborations include the study of Islamophobia in the 2018 mid-term US elections, attitudes toward the resettlement of refugees after the Afghan War, and media interventions to counter Asian hate and to facilitate bystander interventions.